Derrida on Religion

Key Thinkers in the Study of Religion

Edited by Steven Engler, Mount Royal College, Canada

Key Thinkers in the Study of Religion is a series of compact introductions to the life and work of major figures in the study of religion. Each volume provides up-to-date critical evaluations of the place and value of a single scholar's work, in a manner both accessible to students and useful for instructors. Each volume includes a brief biography, analyses of key works, evaluations of criticisms and of overall impact on the field, and discussions of the work of later scholars who have appropriated or extended each key thinker's approach. Critical engagement with each key thinker's major works makes each volume a useful companion for the study of these important sources in the field. Aimed at the undergraduate and introductory graduate classrooms, the series aims to encapsulate and evaluate foundational contributions to the academic study of religion.

This series is sponsored by, supported by the North American Association for the Study of Religion (NAASR), an affiliate of the International Association for the History of Religions.

Published:

Bourdieu on Religion: Imposing Faith and Legitimacy
Terry Rey

Lévi-Strauss on Religion: The Structuring Mind
Paul-François Tremlett

Bastide on Religion: The Invention of Candomblé
Michel Despland

Dumont on Religion: Difference, Comparison, Transgression
Ivan Strenski

Forthcoming:

Rudolf Otto on Religion
Gregory D. Alles

Derrida on Religion:
Thinker of Differance

Dawne McCance

LONDON   OAKVILLE

Published by Equinox Publishing Ltd.

UK: Unit 6, The Village, 101 Amies St., London SW11 2JW
USA: DBBC, 28 Main Street, Oakville, CT 06779

www.equinoxpub.com

First published 2009

British Library Cataloguing-in-Publication Data

A catalogue record for this book is available from the British Library.

Library of Congress Cataloging-in-Publication Data

McCance, Dawne, 1944–
Derrida on religion: thinker of differance / Dawne McCance.
    p. cm. — (Key thinkers in the study of religion)
Includes bibliographical references and index.
ISBN 978-1-84553-275-8 (hb) — ISBN 978-1-84553-276-5 (pb)
1. Derrida, Jacques—Religion. 2. Religion—Philosophy. I. Title. B2430.484M43 2009
210.92—dc22
                        2008028484

Edited and typeset by Queenston Publishing, Hamilton, Canada

Printed and bound in Great Britain by Lightning Source UK, Ltd., Milton Keynes, and Lightning Source Inc., La Vergne, TN

Contents

this book is for Will

Preface and Acknowledgements

Derrida remarks in the last interview before his death, *Leaning To Live Finally*, that survival constitutes the very structure of what we call existence, that: "We are structurally survivors, marked by the structure of the trace and of the testament" (LLF 51). It is this understanding that makes Derrida's writing what interviewer Jean Birnbaum calls a "writing of the inherited promise, of the safeguarded trace, and of entrusted responsibility"—a "writing of survival [*survivance*]" (LLF 30). This writing is affirmative, "an unconditional affirmation of life," and of "life more than life" (LLF 52), never more so than when, as is the case in this interview, it is haunted by an awaiting death. The following book, also haunted by Derrida's death, affirms, is an affirmative response to his work. The book introduces Derrida as a "key thinker" for the study of religion.

I thank my family. I am grateful to editor Steven Engler and the editing and production staff at Equinox Press. Thanks to Amy Becker for Index and proof-reading assistance. And I acknowledge the support of the Social Sciences and Humanities Research Council of Canada, the University of Manitoba, and St. John's College.

Dawne McCance

Selected works by Jacques Derrida

Cited by abbreviation

A   *Aporias.* Trans. Thomas Dutoit. Stanford, CA: Stanford University Press, 1993.

Ad   *Adieu to Emmanuel Levinas.* Trans. Pascale-Anne Brault and Michael Naas. Stanford, CA: Stanford University Press, 1999.

AO   Abraham, the Other. Trans. Michael B. Smith. In *Judeities: Questions for Jacques Derrida,* eds. Bettina Bergo, Joseph Cohen, Raphel Zagury-Orly, 1–35. New York: Fordham University Press, 2007.

AR   *Acts of Religion.* Ed. Gil Anidjar. London and New York: Routledge, 2002.

AS   And Say the Animal Responded? Trans. David Wills. In *Zoontologies: The Question of the Animal,* ed. Cary Wolfe, 121–146. Minneapolis: University of Minnesota Press, 2003.

AT   The Animal That Therefore I Am (More to Follow). Trans. David Wills. *Critical Inquiry* 28(2): 369-418, 2002.

ATG A Testimony Given…. Trans. Rachel Bowlby. In *Questioning Judaism: Interviews by Elisabeth Weber,* 39–58. Stanford, CA: Stanford University Press, 2004.

C   *Cinders.* Trans. Ned Lukacher. Lincoln: University of Nebraska Press, 1991.

CC   *Confessions* and "Circumfession." A Roundtable Discussion with Jacques Derrida. In *Augustine and Postmodernism,* eds. John D. Caputo and Michael J. Scanlon, 28–49. Bloomington: Indiana University Press, 2005.

Cf   "Circumfession." Trans. Geoffrey Bennington. In *Jacques Derrida*, ed. Geoffrey Bennington and Jacques Derrida. Chicago, IL: University of Chicago Press, 1993.

CP   *Counterpath: Travelling with Jacques Derrida*. With Catherine Malabou. Trans. David Wills. Stanford, CA: Stanford University Press, 2004.

D   *Dissemination*. Trans. Barbara Johnson. Chicago, IL: University of Chicago Press, 1981.

DA   Deconstruction in America: An Interview with Jacques Derrida. With James Creech, Peggy Kamuf, and Jane Todd. *Critical Exchange* 17: 1–33, 1985.

DN   *Deconstruction in a Nutshell: A Conversation with Jacques Derrida,* edited and with a commentary by John D. Caputo. New York: Fordham University Press, 1997.

DO   Deconstruction and the Other: An Interview with Richard Kearney. In *Dialogues with Contemporary Continental Thinkers,* 107–26. Oxford: Manchester UP, 1984.

EF   Epoché and Faith: An Interview with Jacques Derrida. With John D. Caputo, Kevin Hart, and Yvonne Sherwood. In *Derrida and Religion: Other Testaments,* 27–50. New York: Routledge, 2005.

EW   "Eating Well," or the Calculation of the Subject: An Interview with Jacques Derrida. Trans. Peter Connor and Avital Ronnell. In *Who Comes After The Subject?,* eds. Eduardo Cadava, Peter Connor, Jean-Luc Nancy, 96–119. London: Routledge, 1991.

FA   Fifty-Two Aphorisms for a Foreword. Trans. Andrew Benjamin. In *Deconstruction: Omnibus Volume,* eds. Andreas Papadakis, Catherine Cooke, Andrew Benjamin, 66–69. New York: Rizzoli, 1989.

FK   Faith and Knowledge: Two Sources of "Religion" at the Limits of Reason Alone. Trans. Samuel Weber. In *Acts of Religion,* ed. Gil Anidjar, 40–101. London: Routledge, 2002.

FL   Force of Law: The "Mystical Foundation of Authority." Trans. Mary Quaintance. *Cardozo Law Review* 11: 919–1045, 1990.

FWT *For What Tomorrow... A Dialogue* (with Elizabeth Roudinesco). Trans. Jeff Fort. Stanford, CA: Stanford University Press, 2004.

G   *Glas*. Trans. John P. Leavey, Jr. and Richard Rand. Lincoln: University of Nebraska Press, 1986.

GD   *The Gift of Death*. Trans. David Wills. Chicago, IL: University of Chicago Press, 1995.

GI   *Geschlecht*: sexual difference, ontological difference. Trans. Ruben Berezdivin. *Research In Phenomenology* 13: 65–83, 1983.

GII   *Geschlecht* II: Heidegger's Hand. Trans. John P. Leavey, Jr. In *Deconstruction and Philosophy: The Texts of Jacques Derrida,* ed. John Sallis, 161–196. Chicago, IL: University of Chicago Press, 1987.

GIV Heidegger's Ear: Philopolemology (*Geschlecht* IV). Trans. John P. Leavey, Jr. In *Reading Heidegger: Commemorations,* ed. John Sallis, 163–218. Bloomington: Indiana University Press, 1993.

GT   *Given Time: 1. Counterfeit Money*. Trans. Peggy Kamuf. Chicago, IL: University of Chicago Press, 1992.

HAS How to Avoid Speaking: Denials. Translated by Ken Frieden. In *Languages of the Unsayable: The Play of Negativity in Literature and Literary Theory,* ed. Sanford Budick and Wolfgang Iser, 3–70. New York: Columbia University Press, 1989.

HT   Honesty of Thought. Trans. Marian Hill. In *The Derrida-Habermas Reader,* ed. Lasse Thomassen, 300–306. Chicago, IL: University of Chicago Press, 2006.

ID   An Interview with Derrida. With Catherine David. In *Derrida and Différance,* eds. David Wood and Robert Bernasconi, 71–82. Evanston, IL: Northwestern University Press, 1988.

K   *Khôra*. Trans. Ian McLeod. In Jacques Derrida, *On The Name*. Trans. David Wood, John P. Leavey, Jr., Ian McLeod, ed. Thomas Dutoit, 87–127. Stanford, CA: Stanford University Press, 1995.

LINC *Limited INC*. Trans. Samuel Weber. Baltimore, MD: Johns Hopkins University Press, 1977.

LJF Letter to a Japanese Friend. In *Derrida and Différance,* eds. David Wood and Robert Bernasconi, 1–5. Evanston, IL: Northwestern University Press, 1988.

MB *Memoirs of the Blind: The Self-Portrait and Other Ruins*. Trans. Pascale-Anne Brault and Michael Naas. Chicago, IL: University of Chicago Press, 1993.

MPDM *Memoires for Paul de Man*. Trans. Cecile Lindsay, Jonathan Culler, Eduardo Cadava, and Peggy Kamuf. The Wellek Library Lectures at the University of California, Irvine. Revised Edition. New York: Columbia University Press, 1989.

MO *Monolingualism of the Other, or the Prosthesis of Origin*. Trans. Patrick Mensah. Stanford, CA: Stanford University Press, 1998.

MS Marx & Sons. In *Ghostly Demarcations: A Symposium on Jacques Derrida's Specters of Marx,* ed. Michael Sprinker, 213–269. London: Verso, 1999.

OAT Of an Apocalyptic Tone Recently Adopted in Philosophy. Trans. John P. Leavey, Jr. *Semeia* 23: 63–97,1982.

OG *Of Grammatology*. Trans. Gayatri Spivak. Baltimore, MD: Johns Hopkins University Press, 1974.

OH *Of Hospitality: Anne Dufourmantelle Invites Jacques Derrida to Respond*. Trans. Rachel Bowlby. Stanford, CA: Stanford University Press, 2000.

OS *Of Spirit: Heidegger and the Question*. Trans. Geoffrey Bennington and Rachel Bowlby. Chicago, IL: University of Chicago Press, 1989.

OTG On the Gift: A Discussion between Jacques Derrida and Jean-Luc Marion. Moderated by Richard Kearney. In *God, the Gift, and Postmodernism,* eds. John D. Caputo and Michael J. Scanlon, 54–78. Bloomington: Indiana University Press, 1999.

P *Positions*. Trans. Alan Bass. Chicago, IL: University of Chicago Press, 1981.

PC   *The Post Card: From Socrates to Freud and Beyond.* Trans. Alan Bass. Chicago, IL: University of Chicago Press, 1987.

PM   *Paper Machine.* Trans. Rachel Bowlby. Stanford, CA: Stanford University Press, 2005.

PSY   *Psyche: Inventions of the Other: Volume I,* eds. Peggy Kamuf and Elizabeth Rottenberg. Stanford. CA: Stanford University Press, 2007.

PT   *Points... Interviews 1974–1994,* ed. Elisabeth Weber, trans. Peggy Kamuf and others. Stanford, CA: Stanford University Press, 1992.

PTT   *Philosophy in a Time of Terror: Dialogues with Jürgen Habermas and Jacques Derrida,* ed. Giovanna Borradori. Chicago, IL: University of Chicago Press, 2003.

R   *Rogues: Two Essays on Reason.* Trans. Pascale-Anne Brault and Michael Naas. Stanford, CA: Stanford University Press, 2005.

RL   Racism's Last Word. Trans. Peggy Kamuf. *Critical Inquiry* 12: 290–299, 1985.

SM   *Specters of Marx: the state of the debt, the work of mourning, and the new international.* Trans. Peggy Kamuf. London: Routledge, 1994.

SP   *Speech and Phenomena: And Other Essays on Husserl's Theory of Signs.* Trans. David B. Allison. Allison. Evanston, IL: Northwestern University Press, 1973.

SST   Some Statements and Truisms about Neologisms, Newisms, Postisms, Parasitisms, and Other Small Seismisms. Trans. Anne Tomiche. In *The States of "Theory": History, Art, and Critical Discourse,* ed. David Carroll, 63–94. New York: Columbia University Press, 1990.

TB   Des Tours de Babel. Trans. Joseph Graham. In *Difference in Translation,* ed. Joseph Graham, 165–207. Ithaca, NY: Cornell University Press, 1985.

TF   To Forgive: The Unforgivable and Imprescriptible. Trans. Elizabeth Rottenberg. In *Questioning God,* eds.

John D. Caputo, Mark Dooely, and Michael J. Scanlon, 21–51. Bloomington: Indiana University Press, 2001.

TS   *A Taste for the Secret* (with Maurizio Ferraris). Trans. Giacomo Donis, eds. Giacomo Donis and David Webb. Cambridge: Polity Press, 2001.

WA   *Without Alibi*. Ed. and trans. Peggy Kamuf. Stanford, CA: Stanford University Press, 2002.

WD   *Writing and Difference*. Trans. Alan Bass. Chicago, IL: University of Chicago Press, 1978.

WM   *The Work of Mourning,* ed. Pascale-Anne Brault and Michael Naas. Chicago, IL: University of Chicago Press, 2001.

Other works by Derrida referred to in this book

——. Aphorism Countertime. Trans. Nicholas Royle. In *Acts of Literature.* Ed. Derek Attridge, 414–433. London and New York: Routledge, 1992.

——. *Archive Fever: A Freudian Impression*. Trans. Eric Prenowitz. Chicago, IL: University of Chicago Press, 1996.

——. At this very moment in this work here I am. Trans. Ruben Berezdivin. In *ReReading Levinas,* eds. Robert Bernasconi and Simon Critchley, 11–48. Bloomington: Indiana University Press, 1991.

——. *On Cosmopolitanism and Forgiveness*. Trans. Mark Dooley and Michael Hughes. London: Routledge, 2001.

——. *Chora L Works* (with Peter Eisenman), eds. Jeffrey Kipnis and Thomas L. Leeser. New York: The Monacelli Press, 1997.

——. *Demeure: Fiction and Testimony; The Instant of My Death* (with Maurice Blanchot). Trans. Elizabeth Rottenberg. Stanford, CA: Stanford University Press, 2000.

——. Economimesis. Trans. Richard Klein. *Diacritics* 11(2): 3–25, 1981.

——. *The Ear of the Other: Otobiography, Transference, Translation.* Trans. Peggy Kamuf, ed. Christie McDonald. New York: Schocken, 1985.

——. *Edmund Husserl's Origin of Geometry: An Introduction.* Trans. John P. Leavey, Jr. Lincoln: University of Nebraska P, 1978.

——. *Eyes of the University: Right To Philosophy 2.* Trans. Jan Plug and others. Stanford, CA: Stanford University Press, 2004.

——. The Future of the Profession or the Unconditional University. Trans. Peggy Kamuf. In *Derrida Downunder,* eds. Laurence Simmons and Heather Worth, 233–247. Palmerston North, NZ: Dunmore Press, 2001.

——. *Geneses, Genealogies, Genres, and Genius: The secrets of the archive.* Trans. Beverley Bie Brahic. New York: Columbia University Press, 2006.

——. Interpreting Signatures (Nietzsche/Heidegger): Two Questions. Trans. Diane Michelfelder and Richard Palmer. In *Dialogue and Deconstruction: The Gadamer-Derrida Encounter,* eds. Diane Michelfelder and Richard Palmer, 58–71. Albany: State University of New York Press, 1989.

——. Languages and Institutions of Philosophy. Trans. Sylvia Söderlind, Rebecca Comay, Barbara Havercroft, Joseph Adamson. *RS/SI* 4(2): 91–154, 1984.

——. *Learning to Live Finally.* Trans. Pascale-Anne Brault and Michael Naas. Hoboken, NJ: Melville House Publishing, 2007.

——. Living On: Border-lines. In *Deconstruction and Criticism,* trans. J. Hulbert, edited by Harold Bloom *et al.,* 75–176. New York: Seabury Press, 1979.

——. *Margins of Philosophy.* Trans. Alan Bass. Chicago, IL: University of Chicago Press, 1982.

——. *Mochlos*; or, The Conflict of the Faculties. Trans. Richard Rand and Amy Wygant. In *Logomachia: The Conflict of the Faculties,* ed. Richard Rand, 3–34. Lincoln: University of Nebraska Press, 1992.

——. No Apocalypse, Not Now (full speed ahead, seven missiles, seven missives). Trans. Catherine Porter and Philip Lewis. *Diacritics* 14(2): 20–31, 1984.

——. *On The Name.* Trans. David Wood, John P. Leavey, Jr., and Ian McLeod. Stanford, CA: Stanford University Press, 1995.

——. *On Touching—Jean-Luc Nancy.* Trans. Christine Irizarry. Stanford, CA: Stanford University Press, 2005.

——. On Reading Heidegger: An Outline of Remarks to the Essex Colloquium. Trans. David Farrell Krell. *Research in Phenomenology* 17: 171–188, 1987.

——. *Politics of Friendship.* Trans. George Collins. London: Verso, 1997.

——. *The Problem of Genesis in Husserl's Philosophy.* Trans. Marian Hobson. Chicago, IL: University of Chicago Press, 2003.

——. *Religion* (edited, with Gianni Vattimo). Stanford, CA: Stanford University Press, 1996.

——. The *Retrait* of Metaphor. Trans. Freida Gasdner *et al. Enclitic* 2: 4–33, 1978.

——. *Resistances of Psychoanalysis.* Trans. Peggy Kamuf, Pascale-Anne Brault, Michael Naas. Stanford, CA: Stanford University Press, 1996.

——. *Sovereignties in Question: The Poetics of Paul Celan.* Eds. Thomas Dutoit and Outi Pasanen. Trans. Thomas Dutoit and others. New York: Fordham University Press, 2005.

——. The Spatial Arts: An Interview with Jacques Derrida. By Peter Brunette and David Wills. In *Deconstruction and the Visual Arts: Art, Media, Architecture,* eds. Peter Brunette and David Wills, 9–32. Cambridge: Cambridge University Press, 1994.

——. *Spurs: Nietzsche's Styles.* Trans. Barbara Harlow. Chicago, IL: University of Chicago Press, 1979.

——. *The Truth in Painting*. Trans. Geoff Bennington and Ian McLeod. Chicago, IL: University of Chicago Press, 1987.

——. *Veils* (with Hélène Cixous). Trans. Geoffrey Bennington. Stanford, CA: Stanford University Press, 2001.

——. *Who's Afraid of Philosophy? Right to Philosophy I.* Trans. Jan Plug. Stanford, CA: Stanford University Press, 2002.

Chapter 1

Introduction

Inheriting Derrida

To begin to read or write a book such as this one is to acknowledge that we are *heirs* of Jacques Derrida. We *are* heirs: this is the way that Derrida himself puts it in *Specters of Marx*, emphasizing the verb *are* in order to make the point that *to be* is *to inherit*, "that the *being* of what we are *is* first of all inheritance, whether we like it or know it or not" (SM 54). What does this mean? In Derrida's sense of the word, inheritance is not about receiving something and having it in our possession to use as we see fit. Inheritance is never "a given," he says. It comes to us as "a task" (SM 54). It comes as an injunction to which we *must* respond. This is the way that Derrida thought of "deconstruction," not as a tool (that we can take from him and use to do this or that with texts), but as a *response*, a way of responding, of saying "*yes*" to the tradition of which he and we are heirs.

We will take this, Derrida's own understanding of inheritance, as our point of departure in this book. The book attempts to introduce Jacques Derrida to students of his work, approaching this work on its own terms, as a mode of responding *affirmatively* to the Western philosophical and religious tradition. For the most part, Derrida referred to this as the tradition or epoch of *metaphysics*. For our purposes in this book, we can take this tradition to have its beginnings with Plato and with the positing of a fundamental distinction between the intelligible and sensible realms. The hierarchical intelligible/sensible distinction, subsequently mediated through Christianity, comes to govern Western thought and culture well into Derrida's day. As a graduate student in Paris during the 1960s, Derrida was one of a number of upcoming intellectuals (Michel Foucault, Gilles Deleuze, Julia Kristeva, Hélène Cixous, among others) who began to question the violence of the hierarchical oppositions that metaphysics puts in place. Derrida understood that, for this and other reasons, inheriting the tradition of metaphysics could not mean blind acceptance of it. He framed the heir's task, then, as involving a *double* injunction. He set out to contest what is deadly in tradition and to affirm what in it *gives life*.

Perhaps Derrida became aware of this double injunction of inheritance while writing his dissertation on Edmund Husserl. In Husserl's phenomenology, Derrida thought, metaphysics had reached a kind of culmination, a full withdrawal of intelligibility from the sensible realm into the realm of the transcendental Idea. But at the same time, Derrida was drawn to such texts as *The Origin of Geometry* because "Husserl there *runs into* writing" (PT 345). In other words, even if Husserl's philosophy represents a high point of metaphysics, it still cannot dispense with the sensible or "written thing" (PT 345). By calling attention to this sensible remainder, to the element that exceeds a metaphysical system and prevents the closing off of the intelligible from the sensible realm, Derrida saw himself as affirming the tradition's "living" part (SM 54). For him, we have suggested, this affirmation was the heir's responsibility.

Things are more complicated than this. But it is fair to say that Derrida's work, his deconstruction, is a response to the remainder that no metaphysical system can successfully either assimilate or exclude. This remainder introduces something heterogeneous to the system, which is one reason why Derrida maintained that an inheritance can never be *gathered* into perfect unity. There is always a "left-over" that haunts dreams of closure and completion. We can call it a remnant or left-over, but only if we acknowledge, with Derrida, that what cannot be gathered does not come after, but precedes the would-be system; and only if we acknowledge that what haunts is already inside the system that would dispel it. An inheritance cannot be gathered for reason of this spectral structure, also because tradition comprises so many voices. For Derrida, as we will see in the Chapter 3 discussion of the *Key Term* "text," and in the Chapter 4 discussion of the *Key Text* "Plato's Pharmacy," not even in the single text of a single author can the heterogeneity of a legacy be gathered into one.

This means that what befalls the heir is an enormous responsibility. In Derrida's words, " 'One must' means *one must* filter, sift, criticize, one must sort out several different possibilities that inhabit the same injunction." Indeed, "[i]f the readability of a legacy were given, natural, transparent, univocal, if it did not call for and at the same time defy interpretation, we would never have anything to inherit from it" (SM 16). Above all, we must remember that, for Derrida, "An inheritance is never gathered together, it is never one with itself" (SM 16).

only close reading
what I generally
Inheriting Derrida 3

Reading

Derrida understood that, in order to take up the heir's injunction and to affirm a legacy's living part, it is necessary *to read* and to study the tradition in question. It is striking that, although so many of his harshest critics did not bother to read his work carefully, he was himself, first and foremost, a close reader. Indeed, Derrida's entire body of work unfolds as reading and response to the work of others. He was not one to "talk off the top of his head," or to stand back some distance removed from tradition and make generalizing promulgations. Because Derrida wrote so closely and comprehensively in relation to thinkers of the Western tradition, his work can prove daunting for students. For the only way to enter Derrida's texts is by close reading of them, and of those to whom his work responds. If there is an available shortcut, the present book does not provide it. Its ambition is to select out from Derrida's oeuvre some terms and texts that will *introduce students to reading* this Key Thinker, and that will suggest something of the contribution his work is making to the study of religion and related fields.

It all begins with responsible reading. If we are to embark on this task on Derrida's own terms, we cannot begin by *gathering* religion into a territory all of its own, or by organizing this book according to the very disciplinary and genre boundaries that Derrida called into question: the boundary between religion and philosophy for example, or between discourses of "truth" and the more "literary" languages of myth, poetry, fiction, and autobiography. Instead, we might begin by noting that Derrida's reading and writing engages philosophers as well as religious thinkers (e.g., Aristotle as well as Augustine of Hippo). It extends to philosophers who are themselves thinkers of religion (e.g., René Descartes, Immanuel Kant, G.W.F. Hegel, Friedrich Nietzsche, Martin Heidegger, Emmanuel Levinas, Paul Ricoeur); to socio-political and critical thinkers whose work has importance within the discipline of religion (e.g., Ludwig Feuerbach, Karl Marx, Walter Benjamin, Jürgen Habermas), and so on. To this list, we could add the mystic texts of Dionysius and Meister Eckhart, the poetry of Friedrich Hölderlin and Paul Celan, the fiction of Franz Kafka and James Joyce, the visual art of Rembrandt van Rijn and Valerio Adami, the linguistics of Ferdinand de Saussure, the anthropology of Claude Lévi-Strauss, *how* the psychoanalytic theory of Sigmund Freud and Jacques Lacan: all of this work, engaged by Derrida, has long been important for scholars and students who take up the always "interdisciplinary" study of religion.

For Derrida, whether the legacy is Greek, Islamic, Jewish, or Christian, violence consists in reducing heterogeneity to unity—a reduction that

sometimes works through a mere hyphen, through the "hyphenated gath-
erings" (Anidjar 2002, 77) of such designations as "Judaeo-Christian." As
John Caputo puts it in *The Prayers and Tears of Jacques Derrida*, "the
violence lies in its gathering into One, into one order, making everyone
speak with one voice, claiming for itself exclusivity and privilege" (Caputo
1997, 271). We will return to this point many times in the following pages,
a point that is crucial to understanding why Derrida is a thinker of *differance*, deferral, spectrality, and supplementarity.

This book

Some great thinkers and writers achieve fame only posthumously. Jacques
Derrida was not one of these. By the time he died in Paris on October 8,
2004 at the age of 74, Derrida's reputation was established around the
world, and not only in English-speaking countries, as one of the "key thinkers" of the twentieth century. After writing his first book-length study on
Husserl in 1954 (*The Problem of Genesis in Husserl's Philosophy*, published in French in 1990; translated in 2003), and then publishing again
on Husserl's *Origin of Geometry* in 1962 (translated in 1978), Derrida put
out three landmark books in 1967 (*De la grammatologie*, translated as *Of
Grammatology* in 1976; *La Voix et le phénomène*, translated as *Speech
and Phenomena* in 1973; and *L'écriture et la différence*, translated as *Writing and Difference* in 1978). From there, he went on to author or co-author
over seventy volumes, along with numerous essays and interviews. Over
the years, he held teaching posts in both France and the United States,
and he lectured again and again in universities and at conferences around

---

The book at a glance:

Chapter 1 Introduction to Derrida and his thinking of inheritance.

Chapter 2 Biography.

Chapter 3 Ten Key Terms.

Chapter 4 Ten Key Texts.

Chapter 5 Derrida's religion, approached through questions that
were put to him over the years.

Chapter 6 Derrida's contributions to the study of religion.

Chapter 7 Some of Derrida's legacies to religion and related
fields.

Glossary

---

the world. His output was prodigious.

In keeping with his own understanding of what it means "to inherit," Derrida's work transforms many of the concepts that belong to the legacy of metaphysics. Even the three 1967 books introduce radical changes to how we think and what we do. Derrida's reading of the tradition's canonical texts continued to challenge academic and cultural conventions over several decades, so much so that Nicholas Royle suggests, we live in a "Derridean epoch." More than those of any other contemporary writer or thinker, Royle contends, Derrida's texts describe and transform the ways in which we think about "the nature of language, speech and writing, life and death, culture, ethics, politics, religion, literature and philosophy. More than any other contemporary writer or thinker, Jacques Derrida has defined our time" (Royle 2003, 8).

After reading *Derrida On Religion*, you should have a good sense of why this is so. This book does not attempt to *present* Derrida. Its work cannot be a matter of *presentation*, for as John Sallis so rightly remarks in *The Verge of Philosophy*, "no one has more thoroughly put in question the concept of presence" than Jacques Derrida (Sallis 2008, 56). The book introduces students *to reading Derrida's work*. We attempt to be attentive to sites in Derrida's work where, again as Sallis puts it, things remain inconclusive, "open to questioning, perhaps even in need of a certain retreat from the question" (Sallis 2008, 58). So much of what Derrida "opened" remains before us, and is yet to be done, a point we will return to in the discussion in Chapter 7 of Derrida's legacies.

Chapter 2 of the book offers a brief biography of Derrida, one that tells us something about how difficult it is, in the manner of metaphysics, to separate a "life" from a "work." The book then moves, in Chapter 3, to a discussion of some of Derrida's *Key Terms*. Chapter 4 attempts an abbreviated reading through some of his *Key Texts*. You will notice, however, that in *both* Chapters 3 and 4, we are reading Derrida, engaging terms through texts, and vice versa, so that as we move along, our chapters interlace. This is as it should be.

Here is a suggestion on how "to use" this book: work through Chapters 2, 3, and 4 prior to reading Chapters 5 and 6. The reason for this is that any understanding of "Derrida and religion" issues presupposes at least some familiarity with his work and his life, such as the early chapters of this book, the discussion of key terms and texts, should give you. Remember that Derrida's approach to religion is integral to his work overall. You cannot bypass this work on a fast-track to religion. Chapter 5 considers Derrida's answer to some questions he was asked about his "atheism," his interest in the name of God, prayer, circumcision, and so on. In mov-

Some tips on how to use this book:

1. Set aside all slogans, catch-phrases, and ready labels that have been attached to Derrida's work and that may have come your way. They will only get in your way in this book.

2. Prepare to read, slowly.

3. Work first through Chapters 2, 3, and 4.

4. As much as possible, *read* Derrida while reading these chapters. Open the texts (his and others) that are under discussion.

5. As you go along, try to appreciate the role of *undecidability* in Derrida's work. Perhaps undecidability emerges more prominently than ever in Derrida when religion is at issue. Reflect on the relevance of undecidability for the study of religion.

6. For Derrida, remember, inheritance of tradition is a task that involves critical choices and ethical decision-making.

ing through Derrida's answers to these questions, Chapter 5 foregrounds what might be the key of all keys to Derrida's work, certainly to his work on religion: the notion of *undecidability*. Chapter 6 overviews Derrida's contributions to religion as a field of study. Chapter 7 suggests what might be some of Derrida's legacies. A brief Glossary follows Chapter 7.

Chapter 2

Biography

Algeria

Jacques Derrida was born on July 15, 1930, in El Biar, Algeria, where he lived until 1949.[1] His parents, Georgette Safar and Aimé Derrida, who married in 1923, gave birth to five children, of whom Jacques was the third. The second child, Paul, died as an infant, a few months before Jacques was conceived (Cf 277). Another son, Norbert, died at two years of age. Derrida's only sister, Janine, was born in 1934. When Derrida's father was only twelve, he began working for the Tachet family, prosperous French-Catholic merchants of spirits and wine. After years of apprentice-ship, Aimé became a sales representative for the Tachets, whose wares he marketed from one grocery story, café, or hotel to another. Derrida said of his father that he was always behind the wheel of a car, sometimes accompanied by Derrida himself. On these travels, he saw his father "in the persona of the petitioner or the applicant: in relation to the clients but also to the boss, whose authoritarian paternalism irritated me as much as his benevolence" (FWT 107). Whether or not it was for reason of his Jew-ishness, Derrida's father suffered humiliation from his Catholic employer, and as if bent by this, "he was stooped; his bearing, his silhouette, the line and movement of his body, it was a though they all bore his signature" (FWT 108). On behalf of his father, Derrida was humiliated in turn, even

---

1. In the interview, "A 'Madness' Must Watch Over Thinking," Derrida notes that his given name was actually "Jackie." He changed it to Jacques only when he began publishing, and for the reason that "Jackie was not possible as the first name of an author" (PT 344). In this interview, Derrida makes an interesting comment on the assimilation that we discuss in the following pages, noting that the Jewish community in Algeria in the 1930s "some-times chose American names, occasionally those of film stars or heroes, William, Jackie, and so forth" (PT 344).

when, with the outbreak of state anti-Semitism in Algeria in 1940–42, the Tachets protected his family, keeping Aimé Derrida in their service,

> whereas they could have simply fired this Jewish employee, as some people were urging them to do, and as they had the legal right to do. I felt humiliated to see him overflowing with respectful gratitude to these people for whom he had worked for forty years and who generously "consented" to "keep him on." (FWT 108)

Derrida grew up experiencing his own share of anti-Semitism, some that was condescending and assimilationist, some that was outright and virulent, both kinds shaping his memory of Judaism, undoubtedly also informing his later interest in the figure of "the other" and his later writing on "hospitality" (see the Chapter 3 *Key Terms* entry on hospitality).

Derrida's life at a glance:

1930	born, El Biar, Algeria July 15.
1949	France, post-*baccalauréat* studies.
1952	Studies at the École Normale Supérieure (ENS).
1954	Dissertation, "The Problem of Genesis in the Philosophy of Husserl."
1957	Marries Marguerite Aucouturier.
1957	Military service, Algeria.
1959	Teaches in Le Mans, France.
1960–64	Teaches at the Sorbonne.
1964–84	Teaches at the ENS.
1966	Johns Hopkins paper, "Structure, Sign, and Play."
1967	Publishes three major books.
1975	Founding of GREPH.
1980	Defends thesis for the *doctorat d'état* at the Sorbonne.
1981	Founding of Jan Hus Association.
1983	Co-founder and director of ICP.
1983	*Art contre/against Apartheid.*
1984	Teaches, École des Hautes Études — Countless travels, conferences devoted to his work, papers, publications, seminars and teaching posts in France and the United States, numerous Honorary Doctorates and other awards.
2004	Death in Paris, October 8.

The young Derrida was indignant at the compliance demanded of, and shown by, Algerian Jews under pressure to assimilate: rabbis wearing black cassocks, and members of the community referring to bar mitzvah as "communion" and to circumcision as "baptism" (MO 54). Derrida was circumcised in this Christianizing, "Catholic," milieu, where, he later explained, "Catholics" was the name given to all who were neither Jew nor Berber nor Arab, even to individuals who were Protestant or Orthodox (MO 52).

In part because of the Jewish acquiescence to "Catholics," Derrida began to think of his community as "disintegrated," fragmented and detached from its own roots: at home in the language of official culture but not in the language of its history, willing to see its heritage "ossified, even necrotized, into ritual comportment," complacent about the "insidious Christian contamination" that was erasing Judaism in Algeria in all but name (MO 54–55). Yet, as if assimilation was not enough, when state anti-Semitism was unleashed in Algeria in 1940–42, intense violence was directed against these Christianized Jews. In 1940, France withdrew from the Jews of Algeria the citizenship that had been granted them by the Crémieux decree of 1870, a situation that extended for two years. During this period, there prevailed "officially authorized, physical and verbal violence, also among children. Declaration of a headteacher in the classroom when Jewish names are called: 'French culture is not made for little Jews'" (Bennington 1993, 326). It was in this climate, at age eleven, that Derrida was expelled on the first day of the school year, so as to reduce the number of Jews enrolled at the *lycée* (PC 87).

Dislocation

Through experiences such as these, endured during the first nineteen years of his life, Derrida developed what he later called a sense of dislocation and of his own "*disorder of identity* [*trouble d'identité*]" (MO 14). He was a Jew whose Sephardic ancestors had emigrated to Africa from Portugal in the nineteenth century, but he felt estranged from the Jewish tradition. He did not learn Hebrew at school—"I do not recall anyone learning Hebrew at the *lycée*" (MO 32)—and he was not taught about his Jewish heritage, leaving him with a feeling of "not belonging in Jewish culture" (ATG 43). To this "radical lack of culture [*inculture*] from which I undoubtedly never completely emerged" (MO 53), Geoffrey Bennington traces the singular character of Derrida's relation to Judaism, already imprinted on him during these early years:

> wound, certainly, painful and practiced sensitivity to antisemitism and any racism, "raw" response to xenophobia, but also impatience with gregarious

identification, with the militancy of belonging in general, even if it is Jewish. In short, a double rejection—of which there are many signs.

(Bennington 1993, 326–27)

As Derrida explained it, however, his *trouble d'identité* had to do with more than a dislocation within and from Judaism. By birth, his identity was multiple: Jewish, Maghrebian (he was a native of northwestern Africa), and French (Algeria was at the time a province or colony of France). Yet he had a sense of not-belonging to any of these:

I am a Jew from Algeria, from a certain type of community, in which belonging to Judaism was problematic, belonging to Algeria was problematic, belonging to France was problematic, etc. So all this predisposed me to not-belonging. (TS 27–28)

His *trouble d'identité* owed at least in part to the "politics of language" (MO 39) in place in colonial Algeria at the time. At the school (*lycée*) Derrida attended, "access to any non-French language of Algeria (literary or dialectical Arabic, Berber, etc.) was *interdicted*" (MO 31), an effective means of denying Algerian culture to French Jews who were also physically marginalized: "For I lived on the edge of an Arab neighborhood, at one of those hidden frontiers [*frontières de nuit*], at once invisible and almost impassable: the segregation there was as efficacious as it was subtle" (MO 37). Neither, as we have noted, was Derrida taught Hebrew, through which he might have accessed the culture and texts of Judaism. "Monolingual," he learned only French, although for him this language, too, came from elsewhere, from "an entirely other place" (MO 42), from a country he did not know and from which he felt doubly estranged through the experience of having his French citizenship revoked. Growing up this way—as a non-Arab in Algeria, a stranger to France whose French citizenship was ablated, an excluded Jew whose tradition was under pressure to Christianize—Derrida acquired a sense of dislocation from any single or singular identity. In later years, he referred to himself as a kind of Marrano, one of those "universal Maranno" figures (A 74) who lives and moves on the border between.

More than an autobiographical detail, then, the "dislocation" of which Derrida writes, for example in *Monolingualism of the Other*, marks the whole of his oeuvre (see Bennington 1993, 327). It links to his sense of the "disjointedness" of time and of history; to his suspicion about claims to self-presence and homogeneity; to his understanding of identity identification as constituted out of, and including, difference, "a difference to itself, a difference with/of itself" (PT 340); and to his contention that an inheritance cannot be fully gathered. In *A Taste for the Secret*, Derrida characterizes "deconstruction" as a kind of dislocation: "it often consists, regularly or recurrently, in making appear—in each alleged system, in each self-interpretation of and by a system—a force of dislocation, a limit in the totalization, a limit in the movement of syllogistic synthesis" (TS 4). Deconstruction "is an attempt to train the beam of analysis" on what "disjoins," on the site of "dysfunction" or "disadjustment" that makes it impossible to close off a system or to gather into one (TS 4). In his own hindsight, Derrida was already disposed toward such deconstructive analysis when he left Algeria for France in 1949 to begin his post-*baccalauréat* studies at the Louis-le-Grand *lycée* in Paris.

Studies in Paris

It was Derrida's first journey across the sea, which seemed to him an infinite space, a chasm, an abyss:

> First journey, first crossing of my life, twenty hours of sea-sickness and vomiting—before a week of distress and a child's tears in the sinister boarding house of the "Baz Grand" (in the *khâgne* of the Louis-le-Grand *lycée*, in a district I have practically never left since that time). (MO 44)

His three preparatory years at the Louis-le-Grand were not easy and not entirely successful academically. "Painful experience," Geoffrey Bennington writes of Derrida's initial year at the Louis-le-Grand: "Uneven and difficult start to studies, except perhaps in philosophy" (Bennington 1993, 328). The second year was no better. "More and more difficult living conditions. Fragile health," and, after a three-month return to El-Biar: "Nervous collapse, sleeplessness, sleeping tablets and amphetamines, has to give up the entrance exam [to the École Normale Supérieure] at the first paper" (Bennington 1993, 328). Derrida recalled this period as "the most difficult, most threatening years" (PT 343). The École Normale Supérieure (ENS) entrance exams and the national *agrégation* competition amounted to a "monstrous torture" for the students involved, and for Derrida in particular, failure would have resulted in his unwanted return to Algeria and to a colonial society that "had become unbearable for me" (PT 343). The experience of the Louis-le-Grand and the ENS was thus an ordeal: "discouragement, despair—failures on the exams themselves: nothing was handed to me on the first try" (PT 343).

Nonetheless, at the end of his third year at the Louis-le-Grand, after passing his entrance examination, Derrida was admitted to the ENS for another four years of study.

> Regular Parisian addresses: boarding hostels at the Lycée Louis-le-Grand (rue Saint-Jacques) and the École normale supérieure (rue d'Ulm), and for more than a year (1951–52) in a minuscule maid's room without running water at 17, rue Lagrange, near the Place Maubert. (CP 290–91)

At the ENS, Derrida became friends with Louis Althusser and had his first meeting with Marguerite Aucouturier, whom he would marry in Boston in June of 1957. They had two sons: Pierre, born in 1963, and Jean, in 1967. From his school days in Algeria, Derrida had been interested in literature as well as in philosophy: "Very early I read Gide, Nietzsche, Valéry, in ninth or tenth grade," and "I dreamed of writing" (PT 341). At the ENS, this plural interest extended, particularly through Derrida's study of Husserl, to include science, as well as philosophy and literature. After travelling to Louvain for research in the Husserl Archives, Derrida wrote his dissertation in 1954 on "The Problem of Genesis in Husserl's Philosophy." This dissertation was his first book-length study, published in French in 1990 and translated in 2003. In 1962, he published on Husserl again, with *Edmund Husserl's Origin of Geometry: An Introduction* (English translation 1978). Judging from the latter text, by 1962, Derrida had realized his dream of writing "between literature, philosophy, and science" (PT 341).

In 1957, during the Algerian war, Derrida returned to the country of his birth for two years of military service (requesting that he not wear a military uniform and that he be assigned to teach in a school for the children of servicemen). He took up his first teaching position at the *lycée* in Le Mans, France in 1959. By 1960, he was teaching at the Sorbonne, moving from there in 1964 to the ENS, where he taught until 1984, when he moved to the École des Hautes Études, also in Paris. In 1980, Derrida defended his thesis for the *doctorat d'état* at the Sorbonne (the thesis was published in a 2004 translation as "Punctuations: The Time of a Thesis" in *Eyes of the University: Right to Philosophy 2*). As a carry-over from his difficult experience as a student, Derrida later said that he never crossed the threshold of the ENS (or any other teaching institution) "without physical symptoms (I mean in my chest and my stomach) of discomfort or anxiety" (PT 343).

Career

Derrida's international reputation took off in 1966 when, on the invitation of René Girard, he participated in a famous conference at Johns Hopkins University in Baltimore, delivering a revolutionary paper on "Structure, Sign, and Play in the Discourse of the Human Sciences" (published in WD 278–93). Following that event, as he remarks in *Counterpath*, his "travels never stopped multiplying and accelerating. Most of them involved, at least as a pretext, some academic invitation" (CP 291). Over the years, he lectured and taught around the world, at universities in Europe and North America, New Zealand and Australia, Jerusalem, Japan, Greece, South America, South Africa, Russia, and so on: the full list is simply overwhelming. The pace was made more difficult between 1968 and 1973, when Derrida "was prevented from traveling by plane by an unsurmountable fear" and had to do all of his traveling by car, train, or boat, even the long trips between Europe and the United States (CP 292). Following the three major books of 1967, translated as *Of Grammatology, Speech and Phenomena,* and *Writing and Difference,* he published continuously, notwithstanding the intensity of his teaching and travel schedules. He held Visiting Professorships at a number of universities, and was granted some twenty Honorary Doctorate degrees.

Despite his intense schedule of traveling, lecturing, and publishing, Derrida was active on a number of other fronts. In an effort both to enlarge the space given by universities to philosophical teaching and research, and to make philosophy more inclusive, he was involved in 1975 in founding the "Research Group for the Teaching of Philosophy" (GREPH: Le Groupe de Recherches sur l'Enseignement Philosophique), which tried to convince the government and citizens of France that philosophy should be taught much earlier than in the last grade of high school, and which promoted the idea of "philosophy across the borders, not only in philosophy proper, but in other fields, such as law, medicine, and so forth" (DN 7; see also Derrida's elaboration on the aims of GREPH in "The Age of Hegel" in *Who's Afraid of Philosophy: Right to Philosophy 1,* 144–149). In 1983, Derrida was one of the founders, and the first director, of a new institution called the International College of Philosophy (Collège international de philosophie), in which "we tried to teach philosophy as such, as a discipline, and at the same time, to discover new themes, new problems, which have no legitimacy, which were not recognized as such, in existing institutions" (DN 7). For one thing, rather than take it for granted that "philosophy," as practiced and taught in an academic institution, necessarily gathers itself in the form of a system, the Collège was directed toward making the idea or project of a system one of its problems (see Derrida's "Sendoffs: for the Collège International de Philosophie" in *Eyes of the University: Right to Philosophy 2,* 216–249). The Collège also set out to challenge the traditional hierarchy of the disciplines, with philosophy at the summit, and to promote research that, while rigorous, might not find support—which might have "no legitimacy"—in an academic institution (PT 109–110). Such initiatives as these should be viewed in conjunction with all of Derrida's publications on the history, structure, and future of the modern research university.

Derrida was also politically active on a number of fronts. For example, in 1981, with Jean-Pierre Vernant and some others, he founded the Jan Hus Association, named after the Czech religious thinker and reformer who was burned at the stake in 1415, and dedicated to assisting dissident or persecuted Czech intellectuals (see Bennington 1993, 334). In the same year, during a visit to Prague to deliver a seminar, Derrida was arrested, imprisoned, and expelled from Czechoslovakia upon his release (see CP 172–175). For another example of his political commitments, Derrida participated in the organization of the exhibition, *Art contre/against Apartheid*, which was held in Paris in November 1983. The exhibition was put together by the Association of the Artists of the World against Apartheid, in co-operation with the United Nations Special Committee against Apartheid. Derrida's "Le Dernier Mot du racisme" (translated by Peggy Kamuf as "Racism's Last Word"), which appeared in the exhibition catalogue, analyses racism "as a Western thing" (RL 293) and approaches apartheid through "a European 'discourse' on the concept of race" that "belongs to a whole system of 'phantasms,' to a certain representation of nature, life, history, religion, and law" (RL 294).

We should mention, as a final note to this brief overview of Derrida's career, that he wrote a number of significant works on visual art (as well as on photography, film, television, and electronic media), and on architecture, often collaborating in transformative ways on projects involving architectural theory and practice. One of these architectural collaborations, undertaken at the invitation of Bernard Tschumi, involved Derrida's work during the 1980s with the American architect Peter Eisenman on the theory and design of a "garden" to be built at Tschumi's Parc de la Villette in Paris. While the garden was never constructed, the chronology, correspondence, theory, drawings, and other texts generated by the Derrida-Eisenman collaboration are published in *Chora L Works* (1997).

Major influences

The trajectory of Derrida's work was in large part determined by the staggering number of others to whom his work responds. Yet, he preferred the word "inheritance" to "influence," the latter assuming too much linearity and continuity, too much of a (father-son) "filiation" from one "great" thinker to another. And, certainly, he did not consider his task as an heir to be the one-to-one *reproduction* of an original, so much as the translation, *transformation*, of the works he read, finding new movement and meaning in a legacy's supposedly fixed concepts. Such transformation is by no means a matter of "anything goes." Derrida draws out his analyses carefully, so as to enable his readers to take up and follow each thread. Neither is Derrida's mode of reading a matter of introducing foreign elements and imposing them on a work: each time he opens another text, Derrida finds sites of dislocation that are already there in the work, even if centuries of interpretation have effectively closed them off. He once referred to this task as one of wielding the "*lever of intervention*" (P 71) in order to release all-but arrested movement, and thereby to limit closure.

In an interview that was first published in 1967 and that appears in translation in *Positions* (1981), Derrida is asked a question of "influence," of the major influences that were operating in *Writing and Difference*. The interviewer, Henri Ronse, suggests that in this text Derrida is "led back" to Nietzsche, Freud, and "always, above all, to Heidegger" (P 9). These three thinkers are of fundamental importance to Derrida, and not only in *Writing and Difference*. Derrida published several times on Nietzsche, for example in *Spurs: Nietzsche's Styles* (1978, French-English version 1979), *The Ear of the Other: Otobiography, Transference, Translation* (1982, English translation 1985), and "Interpreting Signatures (Nietzsche/Heidegger): Two Questions" (in *Dialogue and Deconstruction: The Gadamer-Derrida Encounter* 1989). In addition to "Freud and the Scene of Writing" in *Writing and Difference*, Derrida also published a number of seminal texts on Freud, including *The Post Card: From Socrates to Freud and Beyond* (1980, English translation 1987) and *Archive Fever: A Freudian Impression* (1995, English translation the same year). But as Derrida acknowledges in the interview with Henri Ronse, what he attempted to do in *Writing and Difference* "would not have been possible without the opening of Heidegger's questions," questions that "remain unthought by philosophy" (P 9). The importance of Heidegger applies not only to *Writing and Difference*, but to Derrida's work overall. This is why Leonard Lawlor suggests that "Derrida's thought would not exist without that of Heidegger" (Lawlor 2007, 46–47).

Over the years, then, Derrida acknowledged a number of times that "deconstruction owes a lot to Heidegger" (DN 14). It was Heidegger who, for Derrida, put into question "the major determination of the meaning of Being as *presence*, the determination in which Heidegger recognized the destiny of philosophy" in the West (P 7). But Derrida was not Heidegger's disciple, as such critics as Paul Ricoeur later maintained (see Chapter 6, *Derrida and Religion*). Thus, in the Henri Ronse interview, Derrida goes on to say that despite his "debt to Heidegger's thought, or rather because of it," he attempted to locate in Heidegger's text, "which, no more than any other, is not homogeneous," sites or "signs of a belonging to metaphysics" (P 10). Even, and particularly, in the work of those to whom Derrida's debt is greatest, he attempts "to locate these metaphysical holds" (P 10), in order to set them loose. Nowhere is this more the case than in Heidegger's writing on the animal question, which we consider in the Chapter 4 *Key Texts* discussion of *Of Spirit* and the *Geschlecht* papers.

In that Derrida's task is a transformative one, that of releasing heterogeneity where it has not been acknowledged before, he complicates questions of authorship and of the origin and ownership of ideas, posing for
his readers the question that Nicholas Royle phrases as, "Whose idea
was this?" (Royle 2003, 18). Terms like "supplement," "*pharmakon*," and
"hymen" do not "originate" with Derrida. Rather, as Royle points out, Derrida finds "supplement" in the work of the French novelist and philosopher
Jean-Jacques Rousseau; "*pharmakon*" in the work of the Greek philosopher Plato; and "hymen" in the work of the French poet Stéphane Mallarmé. In Derrida's hands, these terms are not so much "ideas" as they
are the "sites of dislocation" where, as we mention above, totalization,
gathering, is interrupted. As Royle puts it, "Derrida does things with these
concepts, things that are not necessarily attributable to the authorial inten-
tion of Rousseau, Plato or Mallarmé" (Royle 2003, 18). While this is so, we
must also remember that, in Derrida's own account, what he "does" with
"supplement," "*pharmakon*," "hymen," and other similar terms, is to fore-
ground a differential movement that is already at work in the text, even if it
has been masked. The movement is already there, but Derrida's intervention is critical to releasing it, thereby effecting a transformation.

In order to identify "sites of dislocation" in the works of so many of the
major thinkers of the West, Derrida had to proceed painstakingly. His
study of the phenomenologist Edmund Husserl is a case in point. Husserl is one of Derrida's major "influences." In the early 1950s, while a
student at the ENS, Derrida was already seriously involved in Husserl's
work, writing his dissertation in 1954 on "The Problem of Genesis in Husserl's Philosophy." While the dissertation was not published until 1990,
the depth of Derrida's engagement with Husserl was evident by 1962,
with the publication of his incisive introduction to Husserl's *Origin of
Geometry* (translated in 1978 as *Edmund Husserl's Origin of Geometry:
An Introduction*). Included in Derrida's three 1967 books is another study
of Husserl, *Speech and Phenomena*. Of all his publications to that point,
this book comes "first" and is the one "I like most," Derrida says in the
1967 "Implications" interview (published in *Positions*), for it lays out the
privilege granted to the voice and to phonetic writing by Husserl's transcendental phenomenology, which represents "metaphysics in its most
modern, critical, and vigilant form" (P 4–5).

Derrida suggests in the same interview that *Speech and Phenomena*
could be read as "the other side (recto or verso, as you wish)" (P 5) of his
1962 Husserl book. It could also be bound "as a long note" (P 4) to one or
other of the additional 1967 books, *Of Grammatology* and *Writing and Difference*. In other words, the studies of Husserl belong together, and come

"first," in providing the basis for Derrida's overall endeavor. It is in his Husserl analyses, Alan Bass, translator of *Writing and Difference* suggests, that Derrida lays out the theoretical matrix for his entire deconstruction of metaphysics (WD xiii). Just to peruse the Contents of *Writing and Difference* and *Of Grammatology* is to realize how far this "deconstruction of metaphysics" had advanced by 1967. It is also to glimpse how long the list of "major influences" had already grown to that point, including, in addition to Husserl: Martin Heidegger, Friedrich Nietzsche, Sigmund Freud, Jean-Jacques Rousseau, Claude Lévi-Strauss, Ferdinand de Saussure, G.W.F. Hegel, Edmond Jabès, Emmanuel Levinas, Georges Bataille, Stéphane Mallarmé, Maurice Merleau-Ponty, Claude Leibniz, René Descartes, Michel Foucault, Antonin Artaud—and several others.

The list is too long, and things are too complex, to allow for an easy "summary" of Derrida's "major influences." All the more so because his analyses of the works of others proceed in such an intricate way, moving across several languages, knitting something of an ongoing weave from one work and one question to another. These analyses can be difficult-going, even for a specialist trained in several languages. Particularly within the schools of Anglo-American philosophy, the perceived difficulty of Derrida's work has been, and still is, cause for comment, if not consternation. Newton Garver cautions in the Preface to *Speech and Phenomena*, for example, that: "it is wiser not to try a direct translation from Derrida's Heideggerian language into the more straightforward prose of American analytic philosophy" (ix); better to look for another way in. Staying with the 1967 books, and more to the point, Alan Bass writes in the "Translator's Introduction" to *Writing and Difference*, remarking on the issue of languages, that it is a serious question whether the essays in *L'écriture et la différence* can be read in a language other than French, since most of the crucial passages in the book require a translator's commentary (xiv). At any rate, says Bass, "Derrida is difficult to read not only by virtue of his style, but also because he seriously wishes to challenge the ideas that govern the way we read" (xiv).

Let us stay open to these challenges as, in both the *Key Terms* and *Key Texts* chapters of this book, we consider, in more detail, Derrida's engagements with some of his "influential" figures, including: Hegel (*Glas*), Kant ("Faith and Knowledge," "Of an Apocalyptic Tone Recently Adopted in Philosophy,"), Lacan ("And Say the Animal Responded?"), Walter Benjamin ("Des Tours de Babel"), Emmanuel Levinas (*Adieu*, *Of Hospitality*), and others.

Chapter 3

Key terms

Keys to reading

We have noted that in Derrida's work, texts and terms are impossible to separate. This means that the following entries on key terms will necessarily involve some consideration of texts in which Derrida introduces the terms and develops his thinking about them. The chapter introduces only ten terms, although many more could be included and considered as "key" (*aporia, gram, iterability, pas, parergon, supplement*, and so on). The ten terms we discuss belong to the overall weave of Derrida's work. The terms are not static or amenable to "dictionary" definition, as Derrida was inclined to modify them as he went along, or to cast them somewhat differently as the needs of a given analysis required. Remember that he was a close reader whose work developed in response to the work of others. Derrida did not stand back from tradition and generalize about it, and he was wary of terms (e.g., "the subject") that were used in broad and homogenizing ways. To approach a selection of Derrida's key terms, then, it is to forsake generalizing in favor of close engagement with his texts, at least as much as that is possible in an introductory *Key Thinkers* book. It all begins with reading.

Deconstruction

As a participant in a 1994 roundtable discussion at Villanova University, Derrida was asked how what is called "deconstruction" relates to academic programs and academic institutions: is deconstruction "anti-institutional" and the enemy of universities? Derrida's answer to the question describes deconstruction as a mode of inheriting tradition (see the discussion in Chapter 1 above on "Inheriting Derrida"). Deconstruction does not oppose

The chapter at a glance:

This chapter introduces ten of Derrida's key terms, placing them in context, and suggesting why they are key.

1. *Deconstruction*
2. *Phonocentrism*
3. *Differance*
4. *Trace*
5. *Khôra*
6. *Text*
7. *The impossible*
8. *Hospitality*
9. *The messianic*
10. *Autoimmunity*

academic institutions or disciplines such as philosophy, he explains. Rather, deconstruction must be thought of as affirmative, as an affirmation of philosophy and of the philosophical institution. However, in keeping with the *double* injunction that inheritance brings, deconstruction is "not simply conservative, not simply a way of repeating the given institution. I think that the life of an institution implies that we are able to criticize, to transform, to open the institution to its own future" (DN 5–6). Derrida says much the same thing in a 1985 interview, "Deconstruction in America," where, again with reference to the university, about which he wrote and spoke so much, he refers to deconstruction as "a kind of affirmation" that—while it is "traditionalist" in its efforts to preserve memory, history, thought, philosophy, all of which the university is the guardian—"run[s] the risk of raising even the questions that are the most threatening for the university, for the institution, for the solidity of the academic institution, for the respiration of the university" (DA 7). The double gesture is necessary. One must respect both "the tension between memory, fidelity, the preservation of something that has been given to us, and, at the same time, heterogeneity, something absolutely new, and a break" (DN 6). In receiving the gift of tradition, both fidelity and "filial impiety" (non-return of the gift) are implied, Derrida explains in 1983 to Catherine David of *Le nouvel observateur*, and this is particularly the case "with regard to those thoughts to which we owe the most" (ID 81).

In many instances during the years following *Of Grammatology*, when Derrida was asked to explain deconstruction, he referred to a "double," "dual," or "bifurcated" writing, that *on the one hand*, overturns hierarchical oppositions, "brings low what was high," and that, *on the other hand* and in the same process, marks "the irruptive emergence of a new 'concept,' a concept that can no longer be, and never could be, included in the previous regime" (P 42). For example, where the hierarchy speech/writing is concerned, deconstruction, in its first phase, "provokes the overturning of the hierarchy speech/writing and the entire system attached to it" while, in its second phase, it "releases the dissonance of writing within speech, thereby disorganizing the entire inherited order and invading the entire field" (P 42). Whatever the intelligible/sensible hierarchy might be—inside/outside, mind/body, spirit/matter, man/woman, human/animal, and so on—the overturning is necessary because "in a classical philosophical opposition we are not dealing with the peaceful co-existence of a *vis-à-vis*, but rather with a violent hierarchy. One of the two terms governs the other (axiologically, logically, etc.), or has the upper hand" (P 41). Derrida's description of deconstruction as a dual writing is another way of saying that it responds to the dual injunction of inheritance, that it exercises critical vigilance as to the constituting and re-constituting of binary oppositions, and that it thereby *affirms the living* part of a legacy.

Derrida's references to a double gesture, *on the one hand* and *on the other hand*, led some to describe deconstruction all too quickly as a "kind of procedural or methodological schema," a "formula" that could be applied to all sorts of texts (DA 7). But as soon as deconstruction becomes a technique, an instrument to use on texts, it can't work, Derrida cautions in "Deconstruction in America" (DA 7). Deconstruction is not *one*, he says during this interview; it "is neither a system nor a unified discourse" (DA 6). Quite the contrary, what it insists on is heterogeneity, the heterogeneity that keeps unity from closing in on itself and excluding difference to its outside (DN 13). Thus, every time deconstruction is *gathered* into a unified and static super-theory, into a teachable set of theorems, it is displaced by some *deconstruction-ism*. Derrida makes this point in "Some Statements and Truisms About Neologisms, Newisms, Postisms, Parasitisms, and Other Small Seismisms" (SST 88). Deconstruction is *not* a teachable technique, he insists. It is neither a theory nor a philosophy, not a school and not a method (SST 85). Nor is deconstruction "simply a reading or an interpretation," a kind of hermeneutics (SST 86).

As you will have noticed here, Derrida often describes deconstruction by saying what it is *not*. This is the case in his "Letter to a Japanese Friend," where he explains again what deconstruction is *not* or what it ought *not* to be: "not a negative operation," "neither an *analysis* nor a *critique*," "not a method," "could not be reduced to some methodological instrumentality or to a set of rules and transposable procedures," "not even an *act* or an *operation*" (LJF 3). In short, deconstruction is not a tool at the disposal of "an individual or collective *subject* who would take the initiative and apply it to an object, a text, a theme, etc. Deconstruction takes place, it is an event that does not await the deliberation, consciousness, or organization of a subject, or even of modernity" (LJF 3–4).

But what is an event? To begin to understand what this might mean, we need to recall that the term "deconstruction" is itself an *inherited* term, a ("transforming") transposition of two German words used by Martin Heidegger: *Destruktion* and *Abbau* (the latter term is found also in Husserl and Freud) (PT 212). As Derrida explains in his "Letter to a Japanese Friend," with the word *Destruktion*, Heidegger referred not to a negative operation, something destructive, but to his analysis of the structure of the fundamental concepts of Western metaphysics (LJF 1). When Derrida first used the word "deconstruction," he wanted to translate Heidegger's *Destruktion* and adapt the term to his own ends. But translated into French, "destruction" too clearly implied "annihilation or a negative reduction much closer perhaps to Nietzschean 'demolition' than to the Heideggerian interpretation or to the type of reading that I proposed. So I ruled that out" (LJF 1). Derrida came up instead with "deconstruction." The word is French and can be found in the *Littré* dictionary, where one of its definitions is particularly suggestive of Derrida's sense of an "event" that "happens." As cited by Derrida in his "Letter to a Japanese Friend," the *Littré* entry reads this way:

> Se *déconstruire* [to deconstruct it-self] … to lose its construction. "Modern scholarship has shown us that in a region of the timeless East, a language reaching its own state of perfection is deconstructed [*s'est déconstruite*] and altered from within itself according to the single law of change, natural to the human mind," Villemain, *Préface du Dictionnaire de l'Académie*. (LJF 2)

From this *Littré* fragment, we can pull out at least three points: first, deconstruction, like change, is ongoing, something that happens, differently, everywhere and all the time, and that is necessary for survival, for *living on*; second, deconstruction happens *from within* living systems, including languages and texts (and including "text" in the large sense that Derrida gave that word, not just a written text; see the entry on "Text" below); third, and following from this, deconstruction is not an operation, tool, or technique imposed on a work after-the-fact and from without by an interpreting subject or self.

It is fair to say, then, that deconstruction is already going on in the texts that Derrida so meticulously reads, something we will consider more fully in the next *Key Texts* section, in our discussion of "Plato's Pharmacy" for example, where Derrida reads the *pharmakon* (Plato's own term) as deconstructing, from within, the hierarchical oppositions on which Plato's dialogue, the *Phaedrus*, is built. Deconstruction "is always already at work," Derrida says in "A Testimony Given ..." (ATG 50). It is important to note, however, that the "second phase" of the "double gesture" remains necessary in every case. For deconstruction "does not consist only in unveiling and making explicit what is already there. You have to produce new events" (ATG 50). In Derrida's understanding, as we have noted, such transformation is an heir's responsibility, and it is a call to which deconstruction responds.

As a response to the multiplicity, the alterity, that metaphysics, in establishing its same/different, either/or oppositions, has forbidden or repressed, attempted to close off, as such *response-ability*, deconstruction is anything but destructive, and it is certainly not the strategy of nihilism that some have declared it to be. The misinterpretation of deconstruction as negative and as an "orgy of non-sense," more than a simplification, "is symptomatic of certain political and institutional interests—interests which must also be deconstructed in their turn," Derrida says in a 1984 interview with Richard Kearney. "I totally refuse the label of nihilism which has been ascribed to me and my American colleagues. Deconstruction is not an enclosure in nothingness, but an openness to the other" (DO 124). Deconstruction is affirmative: Derrida always insists on this. It is "first of all affirmative—not positive, but affirmative. Deconstruction, let's say it one more time, is not demolition or destruction" (PT 211).

When Derrida first used the term in *Of Grammatology*, deconstruction "was not a master word" (PT 211). He never expected the term to be "accentuated to such a degree by readers," who tended to relate it to the structuralism that was dominant in the 1960s, and to interpret it as a structuralist or anti-structuralist gesture (PT 211–221). Over the years, try as he might, he could not free his work from the term which, as Rodolphe Gasché notes, has become "a catch-word that is now applied to all spheres, to deconstructed stews, deconstructed clothes, and deconstructed office space," and which, when it refers to Derrida's work, all-too-often becomes a label used to close off access and "shelf his thought" (Gasché 2007, 26).

There is a religious heritage, a Judeo-Christian heritage, to deconstruction. Derrida acknowledges this in the 2002 interview, "Epoché and Faith." In response to a question about the relation between deconstruction and Christianity, he points out that the term "deconstruction" has literal links to Christianity through Heidegger's *Destruktion* and Martin Luther's word *destruuntur*. But Derrida adds that his work is neither Heideggerian nor Lutheran, and that the literal links to Christianity do not make that religion more deconstructive than any other. "I can imagine Buddhist, Jewish, or Muslim theologians say-ing to me, 'Deconstruction—we've known that for centuries!' People have come to me from far Eastern cultures telling me just that," Derrida remarks. "And I'm sure that there are Jewish theologians and probably Muslim theolo-gians who would say the same thing. So the fact that deconstruction's link to Christianity is more apparent, more literal, than with other religions doesn't mean that Christianity has a greater affinity with deconstruction" (EF 33).

Remember that for Derrida, no religion is one, a unity from which het-erogeneity can be closed off. And as he indicates in "Epoché and Faith," no one religion can claim privilege in regard to the affirmation, the "yes," of deconstruction, its opening to the other. Nor can "religion" claim to be more deconstructive than, say, "philosophy," or "science." Deconstruction may well be a kind of faith, and Derrida suggests as much in the "Faith and Knowledge" paper that we discuss in *Key Texts* (see Chapter 4). But as John Caputo points out in *The Prayers and Tears of Jacques Derrida*, deconstruction is also "as critical as it is possible to be" of fundamentalist religions that "spill the blood of those who dissent to their 'faith'" (Caputo 1997, 149). Moreover, deconstruction does not identify with any *deter-minable* faith. It never lets "its faith be a faith in a determinate thing or person" (Caputo 1997, 149). We will say more about this in the Chapter 4 *Key Texts* discussion of "Faith and Knowledge."

Phonocentrism

This term, synonymous with "*hearing-oneself-speak*," is definitely a key to Derrida's work. The term figures significantly in Derrida's three 1967 books, particularly *Of Grammatology* and in the Husserl study, *Speech and Phenomena*, "the essay which I like most" (P 4). It remains central to all of Derrida's readings from Plato through Heidegger to Lacan, and it is bound up with his use of several other terms, such as *life*, *sovereignty*, *phantasm*, *auto-affectivity*, and *differance*.

As Derrida explains in *Of Grammatology*, throughout the history of the West, all metaphysical determinations of truth posit an original link between voice and thought. This means that in this tradition, the voice "has a relationship of essential and immediate proximity with the mind" (OG 11). This phonocentric proposition is a (the) fundamental version of the intelligible/sensible hierarchy, for the "voice" that enjoys such privilege in its proximity with the "mind" is fully idealized and interiorized. It is the voice as *logos*, as identical with the idea *before* it passes through the lar-ynx and leaves the mouth as a sensible, embodied speech-sound. This phonocentric idealizing of voice and mind, and their conjunction, sets up an entire system of binary oppositions (interior/exterior, before/after, mind/

body, spirit/matter, speech/writing, and so on).

What Derrida calls *"hearing-oneself-speak"* (*s'entendre parler*) re-fers to this phonocentric idealization of the voice, the voice that is *heard* (understood) in the self's unbroken interiority. Phonocentrism defines the meaning of "self-presence," the claim that the self is fully and immediately related to itself in an original ideality where voice and mind are one; and in conjunction with this, the idea that meaning is immediately present to consciousness. *Hearing-oneself-speak* suggests that being is, first of all, self-relationship. It suggests that the essence of *life* is pure auto-affection, where the self is supposedly fully closed in on itself without need of an outside, "a self-proximity that would in fact be the absolute reduction of space in general" (SP 79).

As a theory of signification, of what Ferdinand de Saussure called the "sign," phonocentrism elevates the signified over the signifier in an intel-ligible/sensible hierarchy (see Glossary). Along the same lines, phono-centrism relegates writing to exteriority, taking the sensible "sign" to be secondary, fallen, finite, "an instrument enslaved to a full and originarily spoken language" (OG 29). As Derrida points out in *Of Grammatology*, the phonocentric debasement of writing often involves a distinction, and another hierarchical opposition, between "good" and "bad" writing. Accord-ing to this distinction, good writing is interior, spiritual, "not grammatological but pneumatological" (OG 17), writing of the conscience or the soul. Bad writing is sensible and instrumental, writing that is embodied and performed by some body, the kind of writing you do with a pencil or pen. Summarizing this good writing/bad writing binary as it is posited by Jean-Jacques Rous-seau in his *Essay on the Origin of Languages*, Derrida notes that:

> On the one hand, representative, fallen, secondary, instituted writing, writ-ing in the literal and strict sense, is condemned in the *Essay on the Origin of Languages* (it "enervates" speech; to "judge genius" from books is like "painting a man's portrait from his corpse," etc.). Writing in the common sense is the dead letter, it is the carrier of death. It exhausts life. On the other hand, on the other face of the same proposition, writing in the meta-phoric sense, natural, divine, and living writing, is venerated; it is equal in dignity to the origin of value, to the voice of conscience as divine law, to the heart, to sentiment, and so forth (OG 17).

Rousseau submits even the Bible to this distinction, for although it is to him "the most sublime of all books," the Bible "is after all a book" (quoted in OG 17).

This distinction between good and bad writing is made by Plato (as we shall see in the Chapter 4 *Key Texts* discussion of "Plato's Pharmacy"), and for this reason, in making it for himself, Rousseau repeats the Platonic gesture, Derrida explains in *Of Grammatology*. Phonocentrism works this way. It recurs again and again throughout the tradition of Western metaphysics—in philosophical, literary, religious, and theological texts. But Derrida insists that "profound differences" (OG 16) distinguish its treatment from one century, figure, text, and context to another, and that these differences cannot be ignored in favor of some gesture of gathering. It is important to note that allowance for such differences marks all of Derrida's umbrella terms, three of which are important here as closely tied to phonocentrism: *logocentrism*, *phallogocentrism*, and *carno-phallogocentrism*. Although all three of these terms are metaphysical constants, differences are found in their treatment from figure to figure and text to text. Keeping this in mind, we will comment briefly on the "general sense" each of these terms has.

Derrida notes in the "Positions" interview (published in *Positions*) that logocentrism is fundamentally an idealism: from the Greek word *logos* (idea, thought, spirit, truth), it takes reason to be ideal (non-material) and, in every case, a cosmic gathering center. Thus, "the dismantling of logocentrism is simultaneously—*a fortiori*—a deconstitution of idealism or spiritualism in all their variants" (P 51). At the same time, "logocentrism is a wider concept than idealism," and "a wider concept than phonocentrism too" (P 51). For one thing, as an entire system of presuppositions, logocentrism involves the notion that reason unveils itself in history, a notion that Derrida analyses in Hegel, for example, in Kant, in Husserl, and to some extent in Heidegger. In Husserl's work, reason "is the *logos* which is produced in history," Derrida writes; it is the *logos* that must then emerge from interiority and take "the detour of *writing*. Thus it differs from itself in order to reappropriate itself*" (WD 166). In the *Key Texts* discussion of *Glas*, we will consider Derrida's reading of this "detour of reason" in Hegel, where logocentrism works itself out as a privileging of Christianity as the "religion of Absolute Spirit" and where, in the process, it shows itself to be a phallogocentrism, that is, a logocentric system that privileges the *phallus* —the male, paternal, figure, as authority, as power and potency. According to Derrida, as we shall see in the discussion of *Glas*, phallogocentrism is, inevitably, carno-phallogocentric: it introjects or incorporates (ingests or "eats") differences in favor of sameness and self-presence, doing so by way of "the mouth," by way of some idealizing "passage through the mouth" (EW 113). It is as if, in metaphysics, "the metonymy of 'eating well' (*bien manger*) would always be the rule" (EW 113).

Differance

In his landmark 1968 essay, "Differance" (which was published in the same year and is included in translation in *Speech and Phenomena*), Derrida points out that the verb "to differ" (*différer* in French, *differre* in Latin) has two seemingly quite distinct meanings. In one sense, it means "not to be identical with," "to be dissimilar from" or "to be distinct from," while in another sense, "to differ" means "to defer," "to delay," "to put off until later," or "to postpone." Both of these senses of "to differ" are at stake in what Derrida calls "differance" (in French, the spelling is *différance*; usually, as in *Speech and Phenomena*, the English translation drops the acute accent). The word "difference" could never refer to both senses of "differing" at once, Derrida explains. Hence, he changes "difference" to "differance," substitutes an *a* for an *e*, deliberately makes "a gross spelling mistake" (SP 131), in order to call up "differing, *both* as spacing/temporalizing and as the movement that structures every dissociation" (SP 130). Difference always suggests movement, *both* the movement "that consists in deferring by means of delay, delegation, reprieve, referral, detour, postponement, reserving," *and* the movement "which produces different things, that which differentiates" (P 8–9).

In the "phonocentrism" entry, we note how, in Derrida's analysis, the tradition of metaphysics takes self-presence to be primary and to be constituted by the unbroken unity of *hearing-oneself-speak*. The change from *e* to *a* already signals the incompatibility of differance with this phonocentric schema, for the change, "put forward by a silent mark," is "purely graphic: it is written or read, but it is not heard. It cannot be heard" (SP 132). But for Derrida, the graphic, the mark, the movement of differance, is not secondary to self-presence, not a "fall" from spirit and interiority into the mundane material world. For Derrida, as we discuss in the entry on *Rogues*, there is no self-present subject who is prior to, and master of, differance. Because there is no layer of pure meaning "whose presence would be conceivable outside and before the work of *differance*, outside and before the process or system of signification" (P 31), what Derrida calls differance cannot be conformed to the presuppositions of phonocentrism.

Neither can differance be understood according to the classical concept of the sign. According to this concept, the sign takes the place of the thing itself, thus defers presence, "to represent the present in its absence" (SP 138). The substitution of the sign for the thing itself is said to be "both *secondary* and *provisional*: it is second in order after an original and lost presence, a presence from which the sign would be derived" (SP 138). Although one could not describe it as an "origin" or a "ground," since these terms belong to metaphysics, difference is more "originary" (OG 23) than the sign, Derrida suggests, and it is "the very basis" on which, and against which, self-presence is announced (P 8). Difference is "primordial" (SP 138), although in saying this, Derrida puts "primordial" under erasure, holds it within quotation marks so as to set it apart from any metaphysical sense of the term.

Derrida concedes in the 1968 essay that thinking about differance is "difficult and uncomfortable" (SP 142). Nicholas Royle calls it outright "mind-boggling" (Royle 2003, 71–71). Part of the "difficulty" has to do with the "primordiality" of differance. We are accustomed to thinking of presence, of unity, first and of differences as secondary, where both the self and the sign are concerned. Furthermore, Derrida's "originary" differance does not simply designate difference or differences in the plural:

> What we note as *differance* will thus be the movement of play that "produces" (and not by something that is simply an activity) these differences, these effects of difference. This does not mean that the differance which produces differences is before them in a simple and in itself unmodified and indifferent present. Differance is the nonfull, nonsimple "origin"; it is the structured and differing origin of differences. (SP 141)

Differance is "before," then, but not according to a before/after concept of time, and not according to a model that would separate "time" from "space," differance as temporalizing ("to differ" as "to delay" or "to detour") from differance as spacing (the interval or distance implied in alterity or dissimilarity).

Trace

Differance, which cannot be thought from within the phonocentric system, marks what Derrida, describing the second gesture of deconstruction, calls "the irruptive emergence of a new 'concept,' a concept that can no longer be, and never could be, included in the previous regime" (P 42). To approach this new "concept," we almost need a new vocabulary, some of which Derrida supplies with the terms he refers to as "undecidables": *hymen* ("neither confusion nor distinction, neither identity nor difference, neither consummation nor virginity, neither the veil nor the unveiling, neither the inside nor the outside"), *gram* ("neither a signifier nor a signified, neither a sign nor a thing, neither a presence nor an absence, neither a position nor a negation"), etc. (P 43). *Trace* is one of these undecidables, inseparable from differance, and just as enigmatic.

A trace never makes itself present. It marks the impossibility of presence and of origin. It marks a distance, a deferral within what we call presence or the present: "the trace is never presented as such. In presenting itself it becomes effaced; in being sounded it dies away, like the writing of the *a*, inscribing its pyramid in differance" (SP 154). This structure of the trace, where what remains is not present and never was, is inevitably an experience of loss and finitude, something that Derrida suggests in many texts, for example in *Cinders*, with all of its references to death, the tomb, the fragile "urn of language" (C 53), incineration, holocaust, and not the least, to cinders as "the best paradigm of the trace" (C 43).

The trace is also what Derrida calls an experience of "the other." Like differance, the trace, he says, "must be thought before the entity. But the movement of the trace is necessarily occulted, it produces itself as self-occultation. When the other announces itself as such, it presents itself in the dissimulation of itself" (OG 47). This element of spectrality is crucial to Derrida's thinking of the trace, and of "truth," of any "manifestation," which is always haunted by an other or by what he calls a "revenant." The other comes *before* the self, in other words, before the speaking subject who then would not begin, or be positioned as, an addressor (author, authority), but as an addressee, one called to respond to the other's announcing of itself, its delivery of the injunction. To think of the trace this way is to recognize that Derrida's challenge to the phonocentrism of metaphysics aims not to reverse speech/writing and related hierarchies, but to open questions of destination and address.

Rodolphe Gasché in *Inventions of Difference* calls the trace a "quasi-transcendental structure" in Derrida's thought, and he suggests that, like differance (*neither* a name *nor* a concept, *neither* intelligible *nor* sensible, and so on), trace is "undoubtedly one of the most difficult problems that Derrida's thought poses for us" (Gasché 1994, 164). Given this, it is best to approach the trace one text at a time, particularly since Derrida's formulation of this particular "undecidable" is intimately bound up with his working through the texts of others, especially of Husserl and Heidegger (for more on this, see Marrati 2005).

Khôra

Like a specter in its comings-and-goings, the other, in announcing itself, does not manifest itself as such, does not present itself as a person or through a proper name. It follows that, as Derrida explains in the "Differance" essay, there is no unique name for what he affirms through his discourse on the differing/deferring movements of the trace. There is no unique name, "not even the name 'differance,' which is not a name, which is not a pure nominal unity, and continually breaks up in a chain of different substitutions" (SP 159). Might this then mean that, with such "undecidables" as trace and differance, Derrida, by way of negations (*neither* this *nor* that), is attempting to describe some supreme and unnamable entity, "some ineffable being that cannot be approached by a name: like God, for example" (SP 159)? Might Derrida's discourse on *undecidability* be a contemporary version of negative theology? In his essay, "How to Avoid Speaking: Denials," Derrida answers the question this way: "No, what I write is not 'negative theology'" (HAS 7). The statement stands as unequivocal. And yet, if Derrida seems at times to qualify the statement by suggesting that, at least, he "would hesitate to inscribe what I put forward under the familiar heading of negative theology" (HAS 8), this would only be for reason of Plato's *khôra* (which some translations spell as *chora*). Derrida's reading of this term extends over many texts and comprises a study in its own right. This entry attempts to deal with the term more briefly than that, and with specific reference to "How to Avoid Speaking: Denials," and to Derrida's essay *"Khôra"* (which first appeared in *Poikilia: Etudes offertes à Jean-Pierre Vernant* in 1987, and is translated by Ian McLeod in Derrida's 1995 volume, *On the Name*).

Derrida's "How to Avoid Speaking: Denials" (which appeared in French in *Psyché: Inventions de l'autre* in 1987, in English translation in 1989) is an extended analysis of three paradigms of avoidance or of speaking in a negative mode. The first is the Greek paradigm, as found in Plato and his idea of the Good that is beyond Being or essence, and of *khôra* that is neither sensible nor intelligible, neither being nor nothingness; the second is the Christian ("without ceasing to be Greek") paradigm of negative theology, as found in Dionysius the Areopagite and Meister Eckhart; and the third comprises the "neither Greek nor Christian" strategies of avoidance that are found in Heidegger's writing on the "passage beyond being." For Derrida in this essay, where these three paradigms are concerned, the Christian negative theologies of Dionysius and Meister Eckhart are the most problematic. To put this problem in summary form, in Dionysius and Meister Eckhart, Derrida finds the positing of a "hyperessentiality" that leads back to the concept of a supreme entity, right back to the name of God, the name that, as it were, such negative theology set out to avoid. Derrida insists that what *differance*, the *trace*, and such terms "mean," while yet "*not* mean[ing] anything" must be thought "'before' the concept, the name, the word, 'something' that would be nothing, that no longer arises from Being, from presence or from the presence of the present, nor even from absence, and even less from some hyperessentiality" (HAS 9).

It is interesting and significant that, in "How to Avoid Speaking: Denials," Derrida reads Plato's *khôra* alongside the tradition of negative theology about which he has serious reservations. He reads *khôra*, however, as having "nothing to do with negative theology" (HAS 39), as a term that cannot be conformed to any theology, ontology, or anthropology, rather, as an *undecidable*, and one that becomes very important for his work overall. Published in the same year as "How to Avoid Speaking: Denials,"

Derrida's essay, *"Khôra,"* unfolds as a detailed reading of the term as it is found in Plato's *Timaeus*, a text that Derrida approaches as caught up in networks of translation and interpretation, and as anything but straightforward. Plato's text offers two accounts of the creation of the universe, in one of which the Demiurge, architect of the cosmos, fashions the visible world as the copy of an intelligible idea; and in the second of which a third element, an inscrutable *triton genos, khôra*, neither intelligible nor sensible, is added to the creation story.

In his reading of the *Timaeus*, Derrida notes that *khôra* appears for the first time right in the middle of Plato's text, like an "open chasm in the middle of the book" (K 104), moreover, that *khôra* figures the place of a bifurcation or opening, an "abyss" between the sensible and the intelligible, between being and nothingness. In all of the ways that Derrida in *"Khôra"* examines Plato's descriptions of *khôra* in the *Timaeus*—as opening, place, receptable, winnowing movement, or "nurse" of becoming and change—he finds that this *triton genos* "provokes and resists any binary or dialectical determination, any inspection of a philosophical type" (K 19). For Derrida, *khôra* (not *the khôra*, which might anthropomorphise *khôra*, turn it into a name) cannot be made to enter a metaphysical schema. As he puts it in "How to Avoid Speaking: Denials," *khôra*, the *triton genos*, "does not belong to a group of three. 'Third species' is here only a philosophical way of naming an X that is not included in a group, a family, a triad or a trinity" (HAS 39; see also the Chapter 4 *Key Texts* entry on *Glas*). *Khôra* does not support a dual hierarchical thinking of sexual difference, and, importantly, it precedes or is "older" than such oppositional concepts (K 106; 116; see also the Chapter 4 *Key Texts* discussion of Derrida's *"Geschlecht* I," which explores such "ancient" and "atemporal" difference in Heidegger).

We will turn to *khôra* again in this book, notably in the Chapter 4 *Key Texts* discussion of "Faith and Knowledge." The latter is regarded as Derrida's most sustained treatment of religion, yet he says of *khôra* there that "[i]t will never have entered religion and will never permit itself to be sacralized, sanctified, humanized, theologized, cultivated, historicized" (FK 58).

Text

"A text is not a text unless it hides from the first comer, from the first glance, the law of its composition and the rules of its game" (D 63). So Derrida opens his essay, "Plato's Pharmacy" (first published in 1968, translated in the 1981 book, *Dissemination*). Derrida's opening should make clear that what he understands as a text is not a fixed or finished ("dead") entity, a depository for the ideas of a mastering subject. A text is marked by *movement*: it dissimulates, hides its logic of play from the reading (and writing) subject and, as if alive, it continues to do so, "remains, moreover, forever imperceptible," Derrida goes on to say. "Its law and its rules are not, however, harbored in the inaccessibility of a secret; it is simply that they can never be booked, in the *present*, into anything that could rigorously be called a perception" (D 63).

In Derrida's sense of a text—which is not confined to the written text, on paper, but which extends to "the world as a text" (CC 41)—we are dealing, not with the representation of presence, but with "the necessities of a *game*," with "paradoxes of supplementarity," and with "force[s] of play" (D 64–65). The linear model of reading must be abandoned, for a text is a "tissue," Derrida says, a "woven texture" that may take centuries to unravel, and that, even then, goes on reconstituting itself, "as an organism, indefinitely regenerating its own tissue behind the cutting trace, the decision of each reading" (D 63). One cannot approach such a text out of the presuppositions of a subject/object hierarchy, "wanting to look at the text without touching it, without laying a hand on the 'object,' without risking—which is the only chance of entering into the game, by getting a few fingers caught—the addition of some new thread" (D 63). To read is to "sign on," to take the risk of "composing with" (D 98) the forces of play. "One must then, in a single gesture, but doubled, read and write" (D 64).

So as "to twist" the dominant conventions of text ("to twist" free of metaphysics), and so as to disturb the idea that paper (a page) is but a flat surface, Derrida, particularly in several of his earlier works, uses visual dislocation, typographic fragmentation, unexpected formats and folds, as if he were staging the *scene* of reading and writing that he so often talks about (for example in "Freud and the Scene of Writing" in *Writing and Difference*). Consider, for example, *Glas* (1974, English translation 1986), written on/as revolving columns; "No Apocalypse, Not Now (full speed ahead, seven missiles, seven missives)" (1984), which takes the form of seven missives or "nuclear aphorisms" that address the nuclear situation and the possibility of nuclear war (see also, "Aphorism Countertime"); and "Living On; Border-lines" (translated 1979), which, for over one hundred pages, borders two texts, "Living On," running on the top of each page, and "Border-Lines," at the bottom of each page, over-flowing the top essay. In a 1997 interview that is published in *Paper Machine*, Derrida indicates, however, that particularly once the computer arrived and challenged us to "invent new 'disorders'" (PM 25), he ceased to be interested in such typographic experiments as the ones he undertook in *Glas* (which was written on a typewriter). Perhaps more to the point, what Derrida understands as the "scene" of reading-writing goes on in every text, even where one would least expect to find it, such as in the text of Plato that Derrida opens in "Plato's Pharmacy." In this essay, Peggy Kamuf reminds us, Derrida is "composing with the most massive force every assembled, at least in the West, against the resources, the reserve, that is, the virtual possibilities of compositional play" (Kamuf 2006, 879). And yet, in "Plato's Pharmacy," Derrida manages to read Plato's text, too, as absolutely heterogeneous, as constituted by differences that are constantly composing with the forces that would repress or annihilate play (D 98). We will return to "Plato's Pharmacy" in the next chapter, for it is a key text, and, it too, a woven texture that may take centuries to unravel.

In Derrida's work, textuality is always at issue, and this means that the issue of translation is never far away. These two, *textuality* and *translation*, are inseparable for him, not only when it is a matter of moving from one language to others (and in Derrida's readings-writings, there are always several languages in play, e. g. Greek, German, French, English), but also when it is a matter of the differences within a given text or tongue. As Derrida suggests in *Aporias*, because the border of translation "passes within one and the same language," the effect of "Babelization" does not wait for a multiplicity of tongues. Hospitality to difference, to "the stranger at home," is the condition of all responsible reading (A 10). In Derrida's practice of reading and writing *as* translation, one takes it upon oneself "to receive, welcome, accept, and admit something other than oneself, the other in oneself" (A 10), thus to keep these differences in play, not to submit what is foreign to the customs police. In line with this, with "Plato's Pharmacy" and its understanding of reading as "composing with," also with Derrida's sense of the double injunction of inheritance, translation should be thought of as *transformation*, regulated and critical, transformation.

We are given a glimpse of what this means in Derrida's essay, "Des Tours de Babel," which begins as a "theorizing" of translation in the biblical tower of Babel story, and then moves to a reading (translation) of another text on translation, Walter Benjamin's "The Task of the Translator." One of the main motifs of Derrida's "Des Tours de Babel" is that of the impossibility of translation, its essential incompleteness: translation as always imperfect, as an experience of "the impossibility of finishing, of totalizing, of saturating, of completing something on the order of edification, architectural construction, system and architectonics" (TB 165). Along with figuring "the irreducible multiplicity of tongues," the tower of Babel story exhibits this incompletion, Derrida suggests (TB 165). Translation is both necessary and impossible, a debt one can never discharge. We might say the same for reading and writing, since, for Derrida, there is always more *(handwritten margin notes at top: Impossible (sans fondement) l'archive)*

than one, and more than one language, implicated in a text.

The impossible

References to experience of "the impossible" occur frequently in Derrida's work, not only when he is discussing the prospect of a perfect translation, but also where justice, deconstruction, mourning, hospitality, and even democracy are concerned. This entry considers justice, deconstruction, and mourning: three sites of the impossible in Derrida's writing. We give a separate entry, the following one, to a discussion of hospitality as one of Derrida's key terms. In the Chapter 4 *Key Texts* entry on *Rogues*, we mention his thinking of democracy as another instance of "the impossible" and as always "to-come."

Derrida provides an important, in-depth discussion of what he calls "the impossibility of justice" in "Force of Law: The 'Mystical Foundation of Authority'." The text, published in *Acts of Religion*, combines two of Derrida's papers, one he delivered at a 1989 Cardozo Law School colloquium on "Deconstruction and the Possibility of Justice," and the other at a 1990 colloquium on "Nazism and the 'Final Solution': Probing the Limits of Representation." In "Force of Law," Derrida explains that while law must have force, else it will not be obeyed—hence the "force of law" in his title, no law without force—the force of law rests on a "mystical foundation." He takes this expression from the sixteenth century French essayist Michel de Montaigne to suggest that, ultimately, the authority of law is without ground. This does not mean that laws in themselves are unjust or illegitimate, Derrida explains, but that in their founding moment (in the inaugural moment of the founding of a nation, for example, where a new system of law is proclaimed and put in place), laws "cannot by definition rest on anything but themselves" and so "are themselves a violence without ground [*sans fondement*]" (FL 242). In part, it is this "mystical foundation" that makes necessary the distinction between law and justice: "Law is not justice" (FL 244). Law is open to deconstruction, Derrida maintains, whereas justice is not: "Justice in itself, if such a thing exists, outside or beyond law, is not deconstructible" (FL 243). This proposition, far from suggesting that we give up on justice or on the differences between just and unjust laws, asks us to recognize that justice *in itself* or *as such* is an "always unsatisfied appeal" (FL 249), a "call" for greater realizations of justice, and heightened sensitivity to injustice, in every case. "Justice is an experience of the impossible," Derrida writes (FL 244), for justice *as such* exceeds any given realization of justice, and thus it "hyperbolically raises the stakes in the demand for justice" (FL 248).

Since it is to this appeal or "this demand for infinite justice" (FL 248) that deconstruction responds, it too is an experience of the impossible. Deconstruction is "a certain aporetic experience of the impossible" (A 15). Derrida recalls this in "Force of Law," making the point that the "one must" of inheritance extends particularly to a tradition's legacy on justice. As he puts it with reference to the tradition of Western metaphysics, "one must [*il faut*] reconsider in its totality the metaphysico-anthropocentric axiomatic that dominates, in the West, the thought of the just and the unjust" (FL 247). In other words, in response to the demand for justice, one must deconstruct the phonocentric concept of the subject that positions man, "preferably and paradigmatically the adult male, rather than the woman, child, or animal" (FL 247), as the measure of what is just and unjust, and that denies, to many humans as well as to animals, the support of law or of right. Considered in this light, Derrida's reading in *Of Spirit* of the question of "the animal" in Heidegger, to which we turn in the next chapter, is an heir's response to the unconditional demand of justice, one instance where deconstruction shows itself to be relentless in its striving for "an increase in responsibility" (FL 248). Remember that, for Derrida, these two realms are not dissociable: the incalculable and impossible realm of justice and the calculable realm of ethics, politics, economics, religion, and so on, where *one must* intervene in response to an unconditional demand for justice (FL 257).

Involved in Derrida's complex analysis in "Force of Law" is his discussion of the "to come" [*à-venir*] of justice, the sense in which justice is always "to come," will always have this *à-venir*, and will always have had it. The *à-venir* of justice has to be rigorously distinguished from "the future," Derrida says: *à-venir* is not akin to messianism; it does not promise that justice will someday arrive. Justice remains an experience of the impossible. And yet, there is an *à venir* for justice and "there is no justice except to the degree that some event is possible which, as event, exceeds calculation, rules, programs, anticipations and so forth. Justice, as the experience of absolute alterity, is unpresentable, but it is the chance of the event and the condition of history" (FL 257).

Mourning is another experience of the impossible, something Derrida reflects on at length in *Memoires for Paul de Man* (English translation 1989). Paul de Man, a European- (Belgium) born American intellectual, a distinguished thinker and Derrida's friend, died in 1983. The book includes lectures Derrida devoted to de Man after his death, and among other topics, it explores memory and mourning. Contemplating the death of de Man, and responding to his friend's work, Derrida asks what *true* mourning is: "*What, then, is true mourning?*" (MPDM 31). Derrida acknowledges that, according to Freud in "Mourning and Melancholia," there are two ways of dealing with the loss or death of the other. The first is mourning, a "normal" response to loss. Its work is accomplished or completed when an interiorizing memory takes the lost one in, so as to make him/her a part of myself. This is what Derrida calls the memory of "possible mourning" (MPDM 35). It contrasts with what Freud terms "melancholia," the second, and pathological, response to the loss or death of the other, where, failing to achieve an interiorizing-withdrawal from the lost object or other, one remains attached and grieving through an open wound. Melancholia fails to bring mourning to a close. But, responding to the death of de Man, Derrida questions whether mourning can ever succeed, whether such mourning is impossible. Where mourning is concerned, he suggests, only failure succeeds. In a 1993 text written in memory of Louis Morin and published in *The Work of Mourning*, Derrida suggests, then, that whoever "works *at* the work of mourning learns the impossible—and that mourning is interminable. Inconsolable. Irreconcilable" (WM 143).

Hospitality

We could say the same for what Derrida calls "absolute hospitality," that whoever attempts it learns the impossible, learns that it exceeds any "pact" of hospitality as right or duty, and "is as strangely heterogeneous to it as justice is heterogeneous to the law" (OH 27). "It is as though hospitality were the impossible," Derrida writes in *Of Hospitality*. This book (published in French in 1997, English translation 2000) combines, on the right-hand page, two of Derrida's lectures on hospitality, "Foreigner Question" and "Step of Hospitality / No Hospitality," and on the left-hand page, a hospitable "Invitation" extended by Anne Dufourmantelle to Derrida to reflect on unconditional hospitality. Such unconditional hospitality would be "the impossible" demand to which deconstruction responds. And it would be in response to this demand, in responsibility to memory, that *Of Hospitality* turns to the legacy on hospitality that is bequeathed to us by the Western tradition.

Of Hospitality examines such issues as the place of the foreigner and the right to hospitality in the Greco-Roman tradition and in the Judeo-Christian one, in historical and contemporary contexts. Derrida suggests that, invariably, Western traditions of hospitality rely on a rhetoric of borders and a thinking that is familial, paternal, and phallogocentric. The tradition puts limits on hospitality, for example, when the Enlightenment philosopher Immanuel Kant (1724–1804), in the seminar "On a supposed right to lie out of humanity" (1797), argues that only conditional hospitality is due to the foreigner. Derrida points out that, in response to the question whether a host should lie to murderers who ask him whether the one they want to assassinate is in his home, Kant answers, "yes," the host should speak the truth, even in this case, and should risk delivering the guest to death rather than tell a lie. For Kant, in Derrida's summary, "[i]t is better to break with the duty of hospitality rather than break with the absolute duty of veracity, fundamental to humanity and to human sociality in general" (OH 71). In some cases, such as the story of Lot and his daughters in the Book of Genesis (19:1ff), or the scene on Mount Ephraim that is recorded in the Book of Judges, the tradition is even more disturbing in the violence it portrays, especially in its violence against women (see OH 151–55).

Of Hospitality should be read in conjunction with Derrida's *Politics of Friendship* (published in French in 1994, English translation 1997). Since *Of Hospitality* reads Sophocles' *Antigone* (and *Oedipus at Colonus*) in relation to "impossible mourning," it should also be read alongside *The Work of Mourning, Memoires for Paul de Man,* and *Glas.* Perhaps most importantly, *Of Hospitality* should be considered a companion text to Derrida's *Adieu to Emmanuel Levinas* (published in French in 1997, English translation 1999). The first part of this book, "Adieu," was delivered at the cemetery in Pantin on December 27, 1995, upon the death of Levinas, while the second part, "A Word of Welcome," was delivered at the Sorbonne a year later at the opening of a two-day "Homage to Emmanuel Levinas." This book, too, is a work of impossible mourning.

Derrida points out in *The Gift of Death*, however, that the word "adieu" can mean at least three things: 1) a salutation, a welcome, "hello," which in certain circumstances in French one says at the moment of meeting, rather than at separation; 2) a salutation or benediction given at the moment of separation, of departure, sometimes forever, at the moment of death; 3) the *a-dieu*, "for God or before God and before anything else or any relation to the other, in every other adieu. Every relation to the other would be, before and after anything else, an adieu" (GD 47). As a meditation on all three of these meanings of "adieu," Derrida's *Adieu to Emmanuel Levinas*, is, as well as a work of impossible mourning, an extended analysis of hospitality as an experience of the impossible. The book is an analysis of the word "welcome" as, Derrida says, Levinas "has put his mark upon it" (Ad 16). This "welcome" implies the kind of hospitable receptivity that says "*yes*" to the other before asking whether the other is a guest or a parasite. "It is necessary to *begin by responding*" (Ad 24). For Derrida, it is the *a-dieu* of this welcome, this relation to the other before and after anything else, that opens hospitality to impossibility and undecidability. This *a-dieu* is not simply a "turn to God" or a "turn to religion" (see Chapter 6, *Derrida and Religion*), to a determinate "God" or a determinate "religion." For in Derrida's reading of "the third" in Levinas (and to some extent against Levinas), the other to which hospitality opens is unknown, impossible to identify, anterior to, before and beyond, religion, theology, philosophy, ontology, any determination.

The messianic

What Derrida calls the "messianic," or "messianicity without messianism," is not, he says, to be confused with religious messianism of any sort, with any specific "horizon of expectation" or with "prophetic prefiguration" (FK 56). The messianic is like hospitality in that it "follows no determinate revelation," and "it belongs properly to no Abrahamic religion" (FK 56). The messianic is "abstract" or "mystical" in the sense of belonging to no determinate orthodoxy, but it is not "mystical" in the sense of belonging to a mystic tradition. Neither is it affiliated with Graceo-Judaeo-Christian "negative theology" (FK 57). What the messianic does suggest is an originary "experience of faith" (FK 56) that consists in "opening to the future or to the coming of the other as the advent of justice" (FK 56). Very much along the lines of what Derrida says about deconstruction and about hospitality, the messianic consists in "opening" and "letting the other come" (FK 56).

Messianicity relates to what Derrida calls the "*à venir*" (*l'avenir*), the "*to-come*" or "*yet-to-come*," the "opening to the to-come" (TS 19). As we note in the above entry on the "impossibility" of justice, the "to-come," for Derrida, is an opening to what is not simply the future, or a future expectation. Unlike "teleology," this opening does not imply foreknowledge of what is still to come (TS 20). Derrida talks about this in *A Taste for the Secret* (1997, English translation 2001) with reference to the "eschatological dimension" of justice. This dimension opens justice to a promise or appeal beyond what it is or can be, and thus makes justice an experience of "the impossible." The messianic suggests a similar openness to a "to-come" that remains indeterminate; that will never become present; and that is not susceptible to ontological or theological "despoilment" (TS 20). Messianicity is a notion of "radical otherness," Derrida suggests, of something that "defies anticipation, reappropriation, calculation—any form of pre-determination" (TS 21). At the same time, respect for this radical otherness is absolutely necessary to realizations of justice in this world. As we suggest in the entry on "the impossible," there is for Derrida an indissociability between the realm of calculation and decision and the incalculable and radical otherness of the messianic or the "to-come."

Autoimmunity

In biological and medical science, an autoimmune condition is one in which an organism directs its defenses against itself, against its own self-protective tissue. From 1994 ("Faith and Knowledge") on, Derrida speaks increasingly of a *general logic of autoimmunity* that is silently at work in every body—whether a self, an institution, or a nation-state—and that exposes that body to threat. We cannot trace the term autoimmunity back to Derrida's earlier work, but if not the term, then the logic, is always there. For autoimmunity comes down to a rhetoric of borders, and is, for Derrida, but another way to analyze the obsessive need to posit a limit between inside and outside; to stave off the foreigner, the enemy, the other; and to protect the interior from difference, from the difference of technology and the prosthesis, even from the difference of writing. The problem is that, since the interior is never pure but already infiltrated by the "outside," the body that would ensure its protection from difference, can only turn against itself. Considered this broadly, the logic of autoimmunity would be central to Derrida's analysis of the "theatre of the prosthesis," from "Freud and the Scene of Writing" to *Archive Fever* (see PM 20, also, for another discussion of "self-immunization," 41–65).

Autoimmunity is important to the political analysis Derrida undertakes in "Autoimmunity: Real and Symbolic Suicides" (in PTT) and in *Rogues* (see Chapter 4 *Key Texts* entry). After the Cold War, he suggests, it became more and more difficult for the world superpowers, particularly the United States, to identify the enemy with a bounded, localizable other, another nation or a terrorist "rogue" state. This changed situation came to a crisis with the events of 9/11, which revealed the terrorist threat to have come from within, from "rogues" who were recruited, trained, and armed *inside* the United States, and who used American planes and communications systems. In "Autoimmunity: Real and Symbolic Suicides," Derrida says of the 9/11 hijackers that they incorporated "two suicides in one: their own (and one that will remain forever defenseless in the face of a suicidal, autoimmunitary aggression—and that is what terrorizes most) but also the suicide of those who welcomed, armed, and trained them" (PTT 95). The situation presents a double bind, threat and promise at once. For if welcoming the foreigner is potentially suicidal, so is an aggressive attempt to make safe the domestic interior, not only by sealing its borders, but also by autoimmunizing itself against the threat that lives within, particularly when, in today's high-tech world, the threat that is interior cannot be removed to some outside.

In "Faith and Knowledge" (discussed at greater length in the Chapter 4

Key Texts entry), Derrida speaks of "this terrifying and inescapable log-ic of autoimmunity" as "indispensable to us today for thinking the rela-tions between faith and knowledge, religion and science, as well as the duplicity of sources in general" (FK 80 n.27). In this text, the media spec-tacle of a papal tour serves Derrida as an example of the contemporary indissociability of religion and science. In today's world, religion cannot manifest itself without taking full advantage of telecommunications and technology—digital culture, cell phones, television, jet airplanes, etc. (FK 61–62). The situation exemplifies what Derrida calls "the *autoimmu-nity of the unscathed*" that will always associate religion and science, at least as long as religion seeks the "self–protection of the unscathed, of the safe and sound, of the sacred" (FK 80), and thus sets its immunizing forces against what is interior to, and indissociable, from it.

Again, for Derrida, there is promise in this "terrifying" autoimmune logic, albeit a promise, a chance, that comes to religion (or democracy, or the self, or the state) as a threat, "threat and chance, not alternatively or by turns promise and/or threat but threat *in* the promise itself" (R 82). This does not mean that all forms of autoimmunity can or should be forsaken. But it does suggest that what keeps the autoimmune community or reli-gion alive is its opening, despite threat, "to something other and more than itself" (FK 87).

Chapter 4

Key texts

Selecting key texts

Given Derrida's astonishing output, the selection of only ten key texts proves even more onerous than the selection of ten key terms. The texts we consider in this chapter are key ones, to be sure. But so are many others we have had to leave out. In some respects, certain texts we do not discuss are more fundamental to his work overall than the ones we include in this chapter. For example, Derrida's early work on Husserl is absolutely important. *The Problem of Genesis in Husserl's Philosophy*, *Introduction to The Origin of Geometry*, and *Speech and Phenomena* are key texts, perhaps *the* key texts to all of Derrida's work, if such a thing could be said. These are texts we touch on in earlier and later chapters but do not include here, in part for reason of the impossibility of condensing them to a summary entry, in part for reason of the difficulty they pose for readers who are, with this book, being introduced to Derrida's work (see, however, the Chapter 3 *Key Terms* entries on *phonocentrism*, the problem with which Derrida deals in the main part of *Speech and Phenomena*, and on *differance*, based on the essay by that title that is included in the book). We have already mentioned that Derrida published three major, *key*, books in 1967, one that was translated as *Speech and Phenomena*, the other two translated as *Of Grammatology* and *Writing and Difference*. The latter book defies summary, as it includes a number of essays (on René Descartes, Edmund Jabès, Emmanuel Levinas, Edmund Husserl, Antonin Artaud, Sigmund Freud, G. W. F. Hegel, and Claude Lévi-Strauss). Although *Of Grammatology* also thwarts summary, this chapter includes an entry on it, necessarily so, as this is the first text in which Derrida offers a prospectus of his project of deconstruction, and it is probably the first text that students of Derrida should read.

The chapter at a glance:

This chapter introduces ten of Derrida's key texts, providing outline discussions of their context and content, and suggesting why, for students
of Derrida and his contributions to religion, these texts are key:

1. *Of Grammatology*
2. *Plato's Pharmacy*
3. *Glas*
4. *Of An Apocalyptic Tone Recently Adopted in Philosophy*
5. *Of Spirit*
6. *Geschlecht*
7. *The Gift of Death*
8. *Memoirs of the Blind*
9. *Faith and Knowledge*
10. *Rogues*

We are suggesting that, for reasons of the length and "introductory" aims
of this *Key Thinkers* book, this chapter does not consider a number of Derrida's key texts. Without attempting to survey these omissions here, we
might suggest some titles that could be "next-steps" for students of Derrida and of his contributions to religion. Derrida's work on Freud is all-but
absent from this *Key Thinkers* book. For a long time, Freud-and-religion
studies had a tangled history, but at least since the 1960s and 1970s,
when Jacques Lacan, Julia Kristeva, Derrida, and others initiated a critical re-reading of it, Freud's work has become impossible for religionists to
bypass. It is hard to overestimate the significance Freud has for Derrida,
and for his thinking (in difference) of such things as repetition, life, death,
memory, trace, and the "unconscious"—an unconscious that would not
be determined by Freudian psychoanalysis as a science or discourse of
truth. Among the essential texts here are "Freud and the Scene of Writing"
(in *Writing and Difference*), *The Post Card*, *Resistances of Psychoanalysis*, and *Archive Fever*.

Necessary reading for students of Derrida and religion are his works
on testimony (*Demeure: Fiction and Testimony*; "A Testimony Given…"),
friendship (*Politics of Friendship*), forgiveness (*On Cosmopolitanism and
Forgiveness*; "To Forgive: The Unforgivable and Imprescriptible"), per-
jury, and sovereignty (*Without Alibi*). His reflections on painting, art, and
aesthetics in *The Truth in Painting*, "Economimesis," and in the interview

"The Spatial Arts," broach some of the great questions of tradition and of the concerns of Derrida's own work. His collaborative works with Hélène Cixous are rich in religious motifs (*Veils*; *Geneses, Genealogies, Genres, & Genius*; which should be read along with Cixous' *Portrait of Jacques Derrida as a Young Jewish Saint*). Finally, we should mention again, as we note elsewhere in this book, that Derrida wrote a great deal about the university and about the institutionalizing of academic study. His work here ties into many of the themes mentioned above and is required reading (such texts as *The Ear of the Other*, "Languages and Institutions of Philosophy;" *Eyes of the University*; "The Future of the Profession or the Unconditional University;" "*Mochlos*; or, The Conflict of the Faculties;" *Who's Afraid of Philosophy?*).

Of Grammatology

This is in many senses an inaugural book, in which, in opposition to the "science of writing" reined in (OG 4) by metaphysics and theology, Derrida proposes his "science of grammatology." He takes the latter word from the *Littré*, where it is defined as a "treatise upon Letters, upon the alphabet, syllabation, reading, and writing" (OG 323 n4). If *Of Grammatology* is such a treatise, it is one without the aspirations usually associated with a "scientific project." For it endeavors to put into question the *logocentrism* (see the Chapter 3 *Key Terms* entry on *phonocentrism*) that governs ("reins in") the thinking of writing in the West, and that invariably takes "truth" as its origin and end. Within a logocentric science, Derrida says, "a certain concept of the sign" and "a certain concept of the relationships between speech and writing, have *already* been assigned" (OG 4). Derrida's grammatological project, such as it unfolds in this book and in his subsequent texts, sets out to examine the logocentric concepts of the sign, speech, and writing across the history of metaphysics. *Of Grammatology* initiates the project and formulates its terms of reference. It is no doubt clear to Derrida, even at this early stage of his work, that his grammatological science will require years of his painstaking work and the concerted efforts of many. We can call grammatology a "science" here, although as Derrida points out at the start, it will never be "able to define the unity of its project or its object," and it will necessarily proceed by "wandering" (OG 4). Something "monstrous," then, as viewed from within the "constituted normality" of logocentrism (OG 5). With this, Derrida had anticipated his critics before they set upon him.

One of the real values of this book for students of Derrida's work is its extended formulation, in Part I "Writing before the Letter," of Derrida's grammatological undertaking, his "project" of the deconstruction of Western metaphysics. In no other text does Derrida both lay out the terms of his undertaking in so full and explicit a way, and put these terms "to the test" (OG lxxxix). This "putting to the test" is Derrida's task in Part II of the book, "Nature, Culture, Writing." As he notes in the "Preface," the second part of the book is "the moment, as it were, of the example, although strictly speaking, that notion is not acceptable within my argument" (OG lxxxix). Derrida's primary example in Part II is Jean-Jacques Rousseau, or what he calls the "age" of Rousseau, as analyzed through one of Rousseau's shorter and lesser-known texts, the *Essay on the Origin of Languages*.

Derrida's reading of Rousseau extends to well over half of *Of Grammatology*. He is concerned not only with Rousseau as "an example" of the way phonocentrism or "phonologism" works, as the debasement of writing and as an ethnocentrism that poses or presents itself as "science," but also with the continuity of the metaphysical concepts of sign, speech, and writing from Rousseau to Claude Lévi-Strauss. Derrida focuses on the "affinity or filiation that binds Lévi-Strauss to Rousseau" (OG 101), but he also "looks back," as it were, to "the example" of Plato, and to the *Phaedrus*, which he undertakes to read in "Plato's Pharmacy." For the debasement of writing that interests Derrida in *Of Grammatology*, "the anathema that the Western world has obstinately mulled over, the exclusion by which it has constituted and recognized itself," extends, he says, "from the *Phaedrus* to the *Course in General Linguistics*" (OG 103). We will turn to Derrida's reading of the *Phaedrus* in our next entry on "Plato's Pharmacy," where we will read "the moment of the example" at somewhat greater length, for the reason that, with Plato and the *Phaedrus*, the "anathema" begins.

In Part I of *Of Grammatology*, Derrida outlines his "theoretical matrix" by way of reading the work of others, numerous others—Aristotle, Descartes, Hegel, Nietzsche, Heidegger, to mention only a few. There is great benefit to reading carefully through these pages, from which we stand to learn

---

In the tradition of metaphysics, Derrida contends in *Of Grammatology*:

"All signifiers, and first and foremost the written signifier, are derivative with regard to what would wed the voice indissolubly to the mind or to the thought of the signified sense, indeed to the thing itself (whether it is done in the Aristotelian manner that we have just indicated or in the manner of medieval theology, determining the *res* as a thing created from its *edios*, from its sense thought in the logos or in the infinite understanding of God). The written signifier is always technical and representative." (OG 11)

---

much about the issues at stake in Derrida's "project," and about his reading as response. From *Of Grammatology*, we learn that logocentrism, not just the purview of philosophers or theologians, extends to the "sciences of man," for example to the anthropology of Claude Lévi-Strauss. More than that, logocentrism is for the West, "*the concept of science*" or of "the scientificity of science" (OG 3). Derrida's reading of "A Writing Lesson" in the *Tristes Tropiques* of Lévi-Strauss demonstrates how the logocentric concept of science debases nonphonetic writing in particular, and how it works as ideology, as "ethnocentrism thinking itself as anti-ethnocentrism" (OG 120). To free grammatology from the "sciences of man," thus to respond to logocentrism in a transformative way, Derrida in *Of Grammatology*, partly with reference to the anthropologist André Leroi-Gourhan, begins to sketch a new thinking of life: history of life as "the history of the *grammè*" (OG 84). This is but another reason why *Of Grammatology* is an essential point of departure for students of Derrida.

Plato's Pharmacy

"Let us begin again," Derrida writes at the opening of Section 1 of "Plato's Pharmacy" (D 65). With the word *again*, Derrida acknowledges that for him, beginning entails a doubling back, a turn, a return; as if the origin were already a re-inscription. As we discuss in the Introduction (Chapter 1), Derrida begins to write by reading, by returning to the tradition that precedes him and by re-inscribing something of an inheritance. "One must then, in a single gesture, but doubled, read and write" (D 64), is the way that he puts it. Derrida's statement might remind us again that, for him, the *one must* of inheritance comes as a double injunction, calling both for a return and for a re-inscription that affirms tradition's most "living" part.

There is no privileged entry point. One must take the risk, Derrida says, of putting a hand in somewhere and getting a few fingers caught (D 63). In "Plato's Pharmacy," Derrida chooses to put his hand into the text, the "woven texture" (D 65), of the *Phaedrus*, a dialogue written by Plato around 370 BCE. In this entry, we will in turn put a hand into "Plato's Pharmacy," second of the ten texts we discuss in this chapter, a text, "an example," we consider here at some length. "Plato's Pharmacy" is an essay first published in French in 1968 and translated in *Dissemination* in 1981. By all standards, the essay is one of Derrida's key texts, and for at least four reasons, it is important for our purposes in this Derrida-and-religion book. First, the essay turns to Plato, whose distinguishing of the intelligible from the sensible marks the beginning of Western metaphysics, the tradition that Derrida attempts to read and reinscribe. Second, in showing how the intelligible/sensible opposition works itself out as a speech/writing hierarchy, the essay locates phonocentrism at the very founding of metaphysics. Third, "Plato's Pharmacy" introduces us to the "*pharmakon*," one of Derrida's "undecidables." This term, like *khôra*, is Plato's. Derrida finds it already there, and already at work, in the *Phaedrus*, but he reads it as deconstructing Plato's intelligible/sensible hierarchy. Fourth, because it takes "composition" as its main concern, "Plato's Pharmacy" provides an indispensable introduction to, and experience of, textuality, as Derrida understands the term.

It is paradoxical that Plato, the father of Western philosophy, is known chiefly as a writer, for in his dialogues, notably the *Phaedrus*, writing is indicted, put on trial, and condemned. This condemnation takes place through the words of Socrates, whom Plato portrays as a teacher. Tradition has it that Socrates wrote nothing at all, leaving Plato to become the "writer," that is, the one who transcribed his teacher's "living speech." Tradition puts Socrates before Plato, speech before writing, not only chronologically, Derrida contends, but—as we note in the *Key Terms* chapter and in the preceding entry on *Of Grammatology*—also as a speech/writing hierarchy, this as Western philosophy's foundational oppositional model of difference, the "anathema" with which Derrida's grammatology contends. In the *Phaedrus*, it is in part by recounting the story of the Egyptian god Theuth, which is a story of the gift and trial of writing, that Plato, through Socrates, debases writing. Plato has Socrates introduce the Theuth story only near the end of the *Phaedrus*, but Derrida argues in "Plato's Pharmacy" that the trial of writing is not a supplement added on to Plato's dialogue: "In truth, it is rigorously called for from one end of the *Phaedrus* to the other" (D 67). To make this case, Derrida reads the *Phaedrus* closely, giving particular attention to the *composition* of the dialogue.

For some twenty-five centuries, interpreters of the *Phaedrus* considered it to be badly composed, written when Plato was either too young or too old to construct a well-made text. In Derrida's description, however, the form of Plato's dialogue is "rigorous, sure, and subtle," its organization a "minutely fashioned counterpoint" (D 67). Of particular interest to us here is Derrida's suggestion that what is "magisterial" about Plato's demonstration in the *Phaedrus* "affirms itself and effaces itself at once" (D 67). Let us follow up on this comment with reference to the *pharmakon*, one of the words that Plato puts in Socrates' mouth when the question of writing comes up, a word that Derrida, in turn, reads as "undecidable." By considering the play of the *pharmakon* both in the *Phaedrus* and in "Plato's Pharmacy," we can learn a great deal about Derrida's mode of reading texts that are foundational for the Western philosophical-religious tradition. We

"Operating through seduction, the *pharmakon* makes one stray from one's general, natural, habitual paths and laws. Here, it takes Socrates out of his proper place and off his customary track" (D 70).

can begin to understand that, in returning to a canonical text, Derrida is actually "taking on the tradition" (to borrow from the title of a book published in 2003 by Michael Naas), grappling not just with a single text, but with centuries of interpretation of it. In the case of the *Phaedrus*, Derrida is grappling not only with the legacy of writing but with the question of legacy itself, with "the very structures of reception, donation, legacy, bequeathing" (Naas 2003, 4) that, as we have said, are at issue in all of his work.

The *Phaedrus* takes the form of a conversation between Socrates and Phaedrus, two characters created by Plato for this dialogue, two fictional figures through whom he represents a number of oppositional distinctions, not only that between speech and writing, but also the related hierarchies of philosophy/literature, city/country, proper/improper, before/after, life/death, *logos/mythos*. Socrates, as Plato's (the philosopher's) fictional philosopher, is portrayed as a man of the city and a knower of truth; older, wiser, and more knowledgeable than Phaedrus, he is also more critically and politically perceptive than the impetuous and sensuous poet who is his interlocutor. As passionate as he is naïve, Phaedrus, the literary figure, is enamored by rhetorical flourish—and he is reliant on writing. Indeed, as the dialogue opens, with the poet Phaedrus leading the philosopher Socrates out of the city into the countryside, the reader is given to know that Phaedrus has a written text concealed under his cloak. Fresh from hearing a speech delivered by the orator Lysias, and now eager to discuss the speech with Socrates, Phaedrus has brought a written copy along, carefully keeping it hidden. Phaedrus needs the written copy because he has not managed to learn the speech by heart: we are only at the opening of the dialogue, and already, writing is shown by Plato to be but a prosthetic device, a supplement for "knowing by heart." We are only at the opening of the dialogue, and already, the supplement has gone under cover; writing is the secret that Phaedrus is hiding, and using to lead Socrates astray. "You must forgive me, dear friend," says Socrates:

> I'm a lover of learning, and trees and open country won't teach me anything, whereas men in the town do. Yet you seem to have discovered a drug (*pharmakon*) for getting me out.... A hungry animal can be driven by dangling a carrot or a bit of greenstuff in front of it; similarly if you proffer me speeches bound in books (*en bibliois*) I don't doubt you can cart me all round Attica, and anywhere else you please (*Phaedrus* 230d-e; qtd. in D 71).

Derrida suggests that by referring to the written text as a *pharmakon*, a substance with enough spellbinding charm to lure even Socrates astray, Plato introduces a suspicion that envelops both books (*biblia*) and drugs (D 72–73). It is interesting and important to Derrida's reading that this association of writing with detour, with the danger of going or leading astray, comes into Plato's dialogue at the point where the story of Pharmacia is introduced, and where, by way of this story, Plato affirms the *logos/mythos* binary. At this point, as the two interlocutors are walking along the banks of the river Illisus, Phaedrus asks whether they have reached the spot where the nymph Orithyia was playing with Pharmacia when Boreas, god of the north wind, swept her over the rocks to her death. Socrates, although he knows the exact location where the story supposedly took place, dismisses such myths as of no interest to a philosopher such as himself. Plato, through Socrates, gives myths a send-off, dismisses them, sends them on vacation, Derrida remarks. But even if he would send myth away, the philosopher needs myth, needs to detour through myth himself in order to state his case, in order to present the philosophical argument that *logos* is superior to *mythos*.

Logos cannot get along without *mythos* in Derrida's reading of the *Phaedrus*. For Plato has to call up the myth of Pharmacia in order to portray writing as *pharmakon*, a potent and dangerous lure. As Derrida reminds us here, "Pharmacia (*Pharmakeia*) is also a common noun signifying the administration of the *pharmakon*, the drug: the medicine and/or poison. 'Poisoning' was not the least usual meaning of 'pharmacia'" (D 70). In the myth, the nymph Orithuia is surprised by death while playing with Pharmacia, while playing, we might say, with a poisonous drug. In Plato's dialogue, it is immediately following discussion of this myth of Pharmacia that Socrates refers to writing (bound in books), as, too, a dangerous *pharmakon*. As Derrida puts it, "[o]nly the *logoi en bibliois*, only words that are deferred, reserved, enveloped, rolled up, words that force one to wait for them in the form and under cover of a solid object, letting themselves be desired for the space of a walk, only hidden letters can thus get Socrates moving" as if he were under the lure of a *pharmakon*. "If a speech could be purely present, unveiled, naked, offered up in person in its truth, without the detours of a signifier foreign to it, if at the limit an undeferred *logos* were possible, it would not seduce anyone" (D 71).

If speech could be purely present, there would be no need for the deadly *pharmakon*. Having gone this far in establishing Plato's suspicion of writing through Socrates' discussion of the myth of Pharmacia, Derrida moves quickly in "Plato's Pharmacy" from the opening scene of the *Phaedrus* —where Socrates, led out of the city along the banks of the river Illisus,

> "Writing is no more valuable, says Plato, as a remedy than as a poison.... The *pharmakon* can never be simply beneficial." (D 99)

has just stretched out on the ground and Phaedrus has taken the text of Lysias' speech out from under his cloak—to the last phase of the dialogue, where another myth is introduced. Once again, in this last part of the dialogue, myth is "called back from vacation" just as the question of writing is brought up.

This time, by way of posing the question of writing, Socrates recalls the myth of the Egyptian Theuth, a demigod to whom the bird called the ibis is sacred and to whom is ascribed the invention of numbers, geometry, astronomy, games of checkers and dice—and above all, writing. As Socrates relays the story, Theuth travels from his home in Naucratis to Ammon to exhibit his inventions and explain their usefulness to Thamus, King of Egypt, who then praises what he finds good, and criticizes what he finds bad, in each invention. Derrida notes, citing Socrates, that when it comes to writing, Theuth assures King Thamus that his invention will make Egyptians wise and improve their memory: "my invention," Theuth says, "is a recipe (*pharmakon*) for both memory and wisdom" (*Phaedrus* 274c–e; qtd. in D 75). But at just this point, right after citing Theuth from the *Phaedrus*, Derrida abruptly "cuts off" King Thamus before we have had a chance to read his reply. "Let us cut the King off here. He is faced with the *pharmakon*. His reply will be incisive," Derrida writes. "Let us freeze the scene and the characters and take a look at them" (D 75).

This stopping to take a look takes several pages of "Plato's Pharmacy," during which Derrida works slowly through various aspects of this scene of the gift of writing in relation to Plato's portrayal of, and struggle with, the *pharmakon*. Plato is always suspicious of writing, and considers it no more valuable as a poison than as a remedy, Derrida argues. "There is no such thing as a harmless remedy. The *pharmakon* can never be simply beneficial" (D 99). Therefore, although Theuth presents writing, the *pharmakon*, to King Thamus as a remedy for deficient memory, Plato attempts to remove any ambiguity this notion of remedy might create. Plato attempts to master the ambiguity the myth attaches to the *pharmakon* "by inserting its definition into simple, clear-cut oppositions: good and evil, inside and outside, true and false, essence and appearance" (D 103). For Plato, as Derrida says, writing is "only apparently good for memory seemingly able to help it from within," whereas in truth, "writing is essentially bad, external to memory" (D 103).

In Derrida's reading, it is through the two myths together, the myth of

Pharmacia and of Theuth, that Plato builds his case against the *pharmakon* of writing. It is not Plato's argument that the *pharmakon* is poison in one myth and remedy in the other, that its meaning depends, as we say, on the context. Rather, writing, the *pharmakon*, is harmful, essentially bad. It is opposed to the good and the true. The trouble is, Derrida says, that Plato cannot master the *pharmakon* with these either/or oppositions. In these crucial pages of his reading, Derrida draws out several instances in Plato where this is the case, where the *pharmakon* will not let itself be governed by binary oppositions. Here is the place to open Plato's work alongside Derrida's, to read with Derrida as he follows the movement of the *pharmakon*. "Its slidings slip it out of the simple alternative presence/absence" (D 109). Where memory is concerned, and where Plato attacks the *pharmakon* as "substitution of the mnemonic device for live memory, of the prosthesis for the organ" (D 108), Derrida demonstrates that what Plato struggles to keep "outside" is "already *within* the work of memory" (D 109). To use the terminology of Derrida's later texts, we might say that metaphysical memory is "autoimmune." It is threatened *from within* by the "danger," the *pharmakon*, that Plato attacks and attempts to relegate to the other side of his inside/outside boundary.

Despite the length of this entry, we have only begun to read "Plato's Pharmacy." When you begin again, "get to thinking," with Derrida, that "something like the *pharmakon*," something "like writing," far from being governed by Plato's hierarchical oppositions, "opens their possibility without letting itself be comprehended by them" (D 103). This "something," a "third" that, like the *pharmakon* or like *khôra*, cannot be comprehended by a dialectical or trinitarian schema, is already a provocation for Derrida in this early essay.

Before leaving the essay, we should mention a matter that is crucial to Derrida's analysis in it: the paternal and familial schema out of which Plato attempts, and fails, to impose his speech/writing, good/bad, *logos/mythos*, interior/exterior, life/death oppositions. As we have already noted, it is King Thamus who, as king of kings, determines the value of the gift he is given by the demigod Theuth, and who, when he depreciates the gift, acts, Derrida says, like a father. "The *pharmakon* is here presented to the father and is by him rejected, belittled, abandoned, disparaged. The father is always suspicious and watchful toward writing" (D 76). Even beyond the *Phaedrus*, Plato "assigns the origin and power of speech, precisely of *logos*, to the paternal position," Derrida contends. This does not mean that *logos* is the father, but that:

> the origin of *logos* is *its father*. One could say anachronously that the "speaking subject" is the *father* of his speech. And one would quickly realize that this is no metaphor, at least not in the sense of any common,

conventional effect of rhetoric. *Logos* is a son, then, a son that would be destroyed in his very *presence* without the present *attendance* of his father.... The specificity of writing would thus be intimately bound to the absence of the father. (77)

We cannot wend our way through the intricacies of Derrida's analysis here, but we must underscore the importance of his calling attention to this fundamental familial, paternal, and reproductive schema, which recurs not only in Plato, but throughout the whole of Western metaphysics. In other words, in the move from a Greek to a Christian legacy, this familial schema carries forward. We turn next to Derrida's *Glas*, which is a study of this schema in Hegel, for whom, as much as Plato, the origin of speech belongs to the father. In Hegel's case, however, the father is not an Egyptian king or god, but Christianity's God the Father, whose *logos* is Christ, the son. From Plato to Hegel, the familial schema is Christianized, but the structure does not change, and, according to Derrida, neither does "the distress of the orphan" (D 77), writing.

Glas

In the above entry, we discuss Plato's positing of an oppositional difference between *logos* and *mythos*, where *logos* is identified with interiority, with the father's (philosopher's, god-king's) living seed (speech, son), while *mythos*, in kinship with writing, is associated with exteriority, supplementarity, absence, danger, and death. Derrida's *Glas* contends with this binary, not by way of its reversal, but by its contamination. Derrida said that *Glas* belongs to neither *logos* nor *mythos*, "is neither philosophy nor poetry. It is in fact a reciprocal contamination of one by the other, from which neither can emerge intact" (DO 122). *Glas* is a mutant, "hybrid" work —Derrida even called it a "monster" (DO 122–123)—so prepare to be taken aback when you first look into the book. Prepare for what translator John P. Leavey, Jr. calls "a strange text. A square text. Upon opening it, you see an odd typography. At least two separate columns confront you, columns erected impassively one against the other, in architectural terms, distyle" (Leavey 1986, 32c). *Glas* deals with philosophy, *logos*, in its left column (references to *Glas* cite it as the "a" column), and poetry, *mythos*, in its right (cited as the "b" column). In the left column, Derrida closely reads the work of the German philosopher G.W.F. Hegel (1770–1831), while in the right, he reads the work of the French poet Jean Genet (1910–1986). Since neither column is intact, however, the book does not simply divide into two, into a Platonic either/or. Each column combines diverse modes and styles of writing and typefaces, and each is cut open by "judas" pock-

> "Is there a place for the bastard in ontotheology or in the Hegelian family?" (G 6a)

ets (cited as "i" in references to *Glas*) that spill diverse bits and pieces of writing onto the middle of the page, leading to leakage, back and forth, between the columns. Needless to say, given this ceaseless crisscrossing movement, *Glas* defies the conventions of linearity and closure that, Derrida says in *Of Grammatology*, belong to "the book" (see "The End of the Book and the Beginning of Writing," OG 6–26).

Notwithstanding its capacity to disorient and dislocate, *Glas* is a magnum opus. Its left column alone is what Simon Critchley calls a "*tour de force* of Hegelian scholarship," an exposition in which Derrida "quotes, often at extraordinary length, rarely making a claim that cannot be textually verified with reference to Hegel's works" (Critchley 1998, 197). So detailed and extensive are Derrida's citations that translator John P. Leavey Jr. saw fit to produce a *Glassary* for readers of *Glas*, a guide-book that, with its thousands of references, is staggering in its own right (see Leavey 1986). In the left column of *Glas*, Derrida's exposition, along with considering the works of several other thinkers, moves in detail through many of Hegel's texts, including: the *Phenomenology of Spirit*, *Philosophy of Right*, *Lectures on the Philosophy of World History*, *Lectures on the Philosophy of Religion*, *Aesthetics: Lectures on Fine Art*, *Faith and Knowledge*, *The Spirit of Christianity and its Fate*. "We will never be finished with the reading or rereading of Hegel," Derrida suggests in the "Positions" interview (P 77). *Glas* certainly makes a case in support of this statement.

We will contain our comments in this entry to the left column only and to its focus on Hegel's works. More specifically, we will limit our concerns to the "familial" schema that, according to Derrida, Christianity takes over from Plato and that, in Hegel, becomes not only a philosophical master concept but also a meta-structure. Derrida's analysis of this all-informing structure makes *Glas* a key text, one that is crucial to an assessment of the implications his work might have for the study of religion. There are many other reasons why *Glas* is a key work. To mention only three of these: it raises the issue of form, and of the importance of form to Derrida's questioning of the concepts of metaphysics; it dramatizes the processes of deconstruction; and, just with reference to the left column, it documents the inseparability of *phonocentrism*, *phallogocentrism*, and *carno-phallogocentrism*, all of these, at least in Hegel, as thoroughly Christianized concepts and structures.

Derrida is much interested in the family in *Glas*, and he even says, early into the Hegel column, that it is the "one thread" on which he chooses to draw. "It is the law of the family: of Hegel's family, of the family in Hegel, of the concept family according to Hegel" (G 4a). In its typographical design, *Glas* might even be a family layout: for on the left is Hegel, the philosophical father; on the right, Jean Genet, a poet who took on his mother's name; and between these two, the father and the mother, is Derrida, the son. In the *Glas* family, however, the son does not return speech, *logos*, to the father, as Plato and Hegel would have it. The son *writes*. Moreover, his writing charts a "bastard course" (G 6a), zigzagging back and forth across the page between the columns, without coming to rest in the unity into which, in Hegel's dialectical philosophy, binary oppositions resolve. One of the meanings of the word *glas*, a tolling bell, suggests this oscillating movement, which sounds a knell for the paternal power of logocentric philosophy. We are not accustomed to reading form and movement in critical texts, but in *Glas* these are essential to the way deconstruction works.

There are many registers of family in the work of Hegel, and so in *Glas*. As one way of "contaminating" the philosophy column, Derrida includes in it biographical details of Hegel's family life, concerning Hegel's bastard son Ludwig, for example, as well as several pages of correspondence pertaining to the relationship between Hegel and his sister Christiane. When Hegel philosophizes about family, however, it is not his own, but the ideal family, Christianity's Holy Family, that he discusses or has in mind. For Hegel, Christianity is the absolute religion, the religion in which the truth and *telos* of history, Absolute Spirit, is revealed by God the Father's incarnation, through the Spirit, in a Son. Hegel models the finite family on the Christian one, and he takes the primary purpose of the family to be the filiation father-son. The woman is necessary to Hegel's family only as a disappearing middle term, the materiality through which the finite father sends his spirit (seed, speech) into nature, in order that it might return to him, raised, in a son. The woman is a *disappearing* middle term in that she does not go on beyond the family to the higher realizations of spirit that are attained by males through education, participation in the nation, and immortalization after death. The woman is contained by the hearth and the tomb. Her role, beyond satisfying the man's needs, is to anoint his corpse and prepare the burial rites that usher him into universality (see, for example, G 131a–149a).

In his *Philosophy of Right*, Hegel describes the family as a determinate

"The spirit is neither the father nor the son, but filiation, the relation of father to son.... The spirit is the element of the *Aufhebung* in which the seed returns to the father.... It is this trinity [this tripleness, *Dreifaltigkeit*] which raises Christianity above the other religions" (G 31a).

> *"Aufhebung* is very precisely the relation of copulation and the sexual difference" (G 111a).

moment in Spirit's journey through history, a moment of the dialectical relief of abstract morality into the syllogism he calls *Sittlichkeit*, ethical life. The family, first of the three moments of *Sittlichkeit*, is itself a syllogism comprising three moments (marriage, property, education of sons). The family syllogism (Derrida calls it the "family circle") comes to a close—the family is *relieved*—when its sons pass beyond the hearth to education and the higher reaches of freedom. Derrida discusses this Hegelian schema of family, modeled on the Christian Holy Family, not just as a determinate moment, however, but as a concept that pervades all of Hegel's dialectical system. Working carefully with Hegel's early texts such as *The Spirit of Christianity and its Fate*, Derrida makes the case that the familial concept was in place long before Hegel had fully elaborated his system, that is, that Hegel's early analyses of Christianity and of the Christian family already provide "the conceptual matrix of the whole systematic scene to come" (G 55a). The concept of family is there from the start, Derrida argues, and it "rigorously inscribes itself" (G 5a) in every part of Hegel's system. Thus, for instance, Derrida finds the concept of family in Hegel's *Philosophy of Nature*, in its descriptions of the difference between animal and plant, and of the passage from animal to human desire (G 110a–117a). Similarly, Derrida reads Hegel's concept of history as familial, as is his concept of philosophy, fine art, education, representation, signification, and so on. "The whole system repeats itself in the family" (G 20a).

As we have suggested, however, in analyzing this pervasive concept of family in Hegel, Derrida is interested in a structure, in the Hegelian dialectic itself as a three-term, "trinitarian," family structure. He argues that, in Hegel, with each dialectical relief (*Aufhebung*), the family circle comes to a close. Put succinctly: "The *Aufhebung*, the economic law of the absolute reappropriation of the absolute loss, is a family concept" (G 133a). One *Aufhebung* follows another, each family circle links into another, in Spirit's return passages through history, making Hegel's philosophy into what Derrida calls a "spiral chaining of the circle of circles" (G 245a). It belongs to this familial structure that, with each closing of a circle, a middle (exteriority, materiality, animality, nature, body, woman) disappears, is excluded, crossed out, consumed. In Hegel's discussion of the family as the first moment of *Sittlichkeit*, the woman who mediates the return passage of spirit to the father through the son, is the middle that gets crossed out. When the familial structure is transferred to Hegel's account of the passage from Judaism into Christianity, "the Jew" becomes the disappearing

---

"Before Christianity, the family had not yet posited itself as such" (G 34a).

---

middle. For Hegel, the transition from Judaism into Christianity is an *Aufhebung*, the raising and relief of a religion of duty into a religion of Spirit, into a religion of incarnation, the first religion of family, the religion of the Holy Family. There is no family before Christianity, no family in Judaism, Hegel claims. In *Glas*, Derrida consistently links Hegel's "searing, hateful portrait of the Jew" (Caputo 1997, 234) to his concept of family and to the familial structure that, which each dialectical relief, crosses out a middle term.

In Hegel's system, although Christianity is the absolute religion, it must still undergo a passage into philosophy, a passage into the Absolute Knowledge (in French, *Savoir Absolu*, Derrida's siglum for which is *Sa*) that only philosophy can attain. Derrida analyzes this passage too as an *Aufhebung* that, in accomplishing the reconciliation of divine Father and Son, relieves the family figure, raises the family, which "is at home only in time" (G 96a), into Absolute Spirit. As a Jew who falls outside the family, Derrida is already excluded from this passage into the Kingdom of Spirit; his bastard writing likewise cuts an inadmissible figure, leaving behind remnant bits and pieces that are released by deconstruction and that cannot be raised. "A sensible remain(s) prevents the three-stroke engine from turning over or running smoothly" (G 252a). There is much to be said, with reference to both left and right columns, about the status of "remains" in *Glas*, about the deconstructive significance of the "after effect" that is in excess of, and cannot be assimilated by, the Hegelian dialectic.

Of particular importance in this regard is Derrida's reading of Antigone, sister of Polynices in the family tragedy, *Antigone*, written by Sophocles. Hegel praises this tragic drama, not only as the story of a family, but also, through the opposition of Creon and Antigone, as enacting the dialectical ("familial") passage to a higher order realization of Spirit. In this reconciliation of Spirit, Antigone, the woman, would be crossed out as she meets her demise in the tomb. In his reading of Hegel, however, Derrida suggests that Antigone remains. She is "a figure inadmissible in the system," is "what cannot be assimilated, the absolute indigestible" (G 151a), and precisely as such, Derrida says, she plays "a fundamental role in the system" (G 151a) and even "assures the system's space of possibility" (G 162a).

Of an apocalyptic tone recently adopted in philosophy

One of the issues at stake in the exchange between Derrida and John Searle over Anglo-American speech-act theory (the main texts of which are published or summarized in *Limited INC*) concerns the kind of writing that is "proper" to philosophy and appropriate to "serious" academic discussion. What distinguishes true philosophy from what poses as such, but is only a discourse of "tricks and gimmicks," the "false" philosophy that some critics accused Derrida of at the time of the Cambridge University honorary degree controversy (see PT 399–421)? The claim that true philosophy can and must be distinguished from false pretenders is made by Immanuel Kant in a late essay, "Of an Overlordly Tone Recently Adopted in Philosophy" (1796), the text to which Derrida responds in "Of an Apocalyptic Tone Recently Adopted in Philosophy" (an essay he delivered at a 1980 conference on his work, published in translation in 1982). In this entry, we consider Derrida's essay as a key text that "puts to the test" a number of his critical concepts, including his concept of textuality, which here meets its match in the biblical Book of Revelations (for a more extended discussion of Derrida's essay, see McCance 1996, 23–41). This text is also a significant key to the "call" to which deconstruction responds.

In "Of an Overlordly Tone Recently Adopted in Philosophy," Kant denounces the contamination of philosophy by what he calls "mystagogy." He rails against "mystagogues"—poets, enthusiasts, mystics, cult-followers, dramatists, all who presume to speak in the name of philosophy, who proffer supernatural or intuitive knowledge as a supplement or surrogate of rational faith. Mystagogues blur the distinction between *logos* and *mythos*, which is cause for some alarm. Indeed, Kant says, failure to distinguish between the voice of moral reason and the voice of the oracle leads to *Verstimmung* (discord, disorder, upset), to the untuning (*Verstimmen*) of philosophy. What Kant attempts is the *gathering* of tone. "Isn't the dream or the ideal of philosophic discourse, of philosophical address [*allocution*], and of the writing supposed to represent that address, isn't it to make the tonal difference inaudible—and with it a whole desire, affect, or scene that works (over) the concept as contraband?," Derrida asks. "Through what is called neutrality of tone, philosophical discourse must also guarantee the neutrality or at least the imperturbable serenity that should accompany the relation to the true and the universal" (OAT 66). For Kant, the mystagogic tone marks a deviation from the norm of philosophical address, Derrida says: "the tonal difference does not pass for the essentially philosophic" (OAT 67).

Kant is concerned in his tract not with the pure phenomenon of tonality,

"The *double bind* of filiation: Kant has the 'devilish job' of 'distinguishing between the good Plato and the bad Plato, the true and the false, his authentic writings and his more or less reliable and apocryphal ones. That is to say, his Letters." (OAT 73)

Derrida suggests, so much as with a manner or mannerism of taking on airs, "the grand air of those pretentious people who elevate their voice" (OAT 70), or who "place themselves out of the common" (69), the presumption of the mystagogic impostors. Thus, Kant does not "indict the pitch or loftiness of the overlordly tone when it is just, natural, or legitimate," but only "takes aim at raising the tone when an upstart [*parvenu*] authorizes himself in this by giving himself airs and by erecting usurped signs of social membership" (OAT 70). Kant's argument, in the various ways it is posed, constitutes a same/different, inside/outside hierarchy. He wants to distinguish the intelligible from the sensible realm, thus to draw a clear boundary between philosophy and poetry, between concept and metaphor (on the concept/metaphor distinction, see the Chapter 6 *Derrida and Religion* entry on Derrida's encounter with Paul Ricoeur). "Kant does not doubt this: the new preachers need to pervert philosophy into poetry in order to give themselves grand airs, to occupy through simulacrum and mimicry the place of the great, to usurp thus a power of symbolic essence" (OAT 77). Kant is so insistent on demarcating true philosophy from poetic schemas that, Derrida notes, he must draw a line even through Plato, so as to divide the father of philosophy from Plato, "the father of the delirium," the assumed letter-writer (OAT 73–74).

In part, Derrida's reading of Kant's "Of an Overlordly Tone Recently Adopted in Philosophy" proceeds as an "apocalypse" ("unveiling") of the binary oppositions through which Kant builds his case against the mystagogues and the danger they pose: threatening the "emasculation" of reason, perhaps even the death (the end, the apocalypse) of true philosophy. Derrida's essay draws out the "familial" structure that operates in Kant's tract, that turns the intelligible/sensible opposition into an account of dual sexual difference, and that, in the "truce" Kant proposes to the mystagogues, makes the body of woman (of the goddess Isis) an "*inadmissible*," an "excluded middle" (OAT 79; see the entry in this chapter on *Glas*). But in the process of examining this oppositional schema, Derrida reads with an ear to the tonal differences that even Kant is unable to successfully gather. Of course, Kant's text is a lampoon, Derrida notes. It avails of the devices of metaphor, sarcasm, satire, rhetorical staging, and is thus "carried away" by the poetical itself. Kant's text is also an instance of the apocalyptic genre. It is one of many eschatological discourses (Hegelian, Marxist, Nietzschean, etc.) that modernity has produced, each form "a going-one-better" than the last (OAT 80). Derrida suggests that a limit case of the eschatological genre, also a fundamental source text for it, is the Johannine Apocalypse. The "spectrography of the tone and of the changing of tone" (OAT 93) that he reads in this text attests to the futility

> "*'Come'* is *only* derivable, absolutely derivable, but only from the other."
>
> (OAT 94).

of attempts to stop ears against the other, to gather or to bring to a close
(see Fenves 1993, 1–48).

Derrida is particularly interested in the "Come" that sounds in the Book of
Revelation each time the Lamb opens one of the seals, again in Chapters
17 and 21, and in a chorus of final repetitions that occurs when John receives from the angelic messenger the order not to seal his text. The Johannine "Come" does not come from John, who, though he is the writer, is not
the author of the biblical Apocalypse. For when John speaks, Derrida points
out, he speaks by citing another, Jesus; and when he writes, he "appears
to transcribe what he says by recounting that he cites Jesus the moment
Jesus dictates to him to write" (OAT 85). John does not write as a determinable sender or author, then, but as one who responds: "'write, *grapson*'....
Write and send, dictates the voice come from behind, in the back of John"
(OAT 85–86). Even before this narrative scene, there occurs in the Apocalypse what Derrida calls "a kind of title or name tag [*médaille*] come from
one knows not where" (OAT 86), which indicates that John receives his
dictation through the medium of an angelic messenger, that the apocalyptic
dispatch is thus bound to yet another voice. With each repetition of "Come,"
the dispatches and messengers increase, leading to "an interlacing of voices and *envois* in the dictated or addressed writing" (OAT 87).

What the "Come" of the biblical Apocalypse "reveals" to the apocalyptic
genre today, Derrida suggests, is a "transcendental structure" (OAT 87)
that is the condition, not only of apocalyptic writing, but of discourse in
general. "Come from the other already as a response and a citation without past present," the "Come" to which deconstruction responds in the
Apocalypse does not belong to an "I" or a "self" or a system. "It is a drift
[*une dérive*] underivable from the identity of a determination" (OAT 94).
It is necessary to reflect on this "Come" in relation to everything Derrida
writes on inheritance, responsibility, hospitality, the "third," the pharmakon,
the impossible, *khôra*, and the structure of "reflecting faith."

Of Spirit

In 1987, Derrida published *De l'esprit: Heidegger et la Question*, which was
delivered as a lecture in March of that year at the *Collège international de
philosophie* in Paris, and which took an earlier and shorter outline form in a
1986 paper, "On Reading Heidegger: An Outline of Remarks to the Essex
Colloquium." *De l'esprit*, translated in 1989 as *Of Spirit: Heidegger and the*

Question, turns around four "open questions," questions that were opened by Martin Heidegger (1889–1976) and that remain open with regard to his work, "four threads" that were "left hanging, uncertain, still in movement," thus for Derrida, "*yet to come* in Heidegger's text" (OS 7). These threads, Derrida says, interlace, tie, even *knot*, together in Heidegger's work. They are: first, the privilege of the *question* and of questioning; second, the privilege of *essence*, particularly in Heidegger's account of the essence of technology; third, the discourse on the *animal* and on life; fourth, the thinking of *epochality*. By Derrida's standards, *Of Spirit* is not a long text, running to just over one hundred pages, as it moves through the four threads. The book is required reading for students of religion, and not the least for its probing of what it means to inherit the Platonic and Christian legacy of *spirit*; also for its consideration of "the animal" question in Heidegger (this, in its ties to spirit, as site of the political in Heidegger's texts); and for another instance of Derrida's probing of the "promise" to which language opens, "a *yes* before all opposition of *yes* and *no*" (OS 94).

It is with spirit that Derrida's analysis of the four threads begins, with spirit (*Geist*), as a word that Heidegger tries to avoid in *Being and Time*. This text (published in German in 1927, translated in 1962) became Heidegger's most celebrated work and one of the landmark books of the twentieth century. In the book, Heidegger attempts an inquiry into the meaning of Being, an inquiry that, in its mode of questioning Being, would not be beholden to metaphysics. Wanting to distinguish his mode of inquiry from the approaches of Descartes, Hegel, and Husserl, and from all metaphysical philosophies that, in binary fashion, oppose intelligible to sensible, spirit to matter, Heidegger introduces his work as an *existential analysis* that proceeds, not as a thinking of essence, but as a questioning of existence (OS 21). So as to remove his existential analysis from the soul and body, spirit and matter, oppositions of metaphysics, Heidegger determines to steer clear of the word and the concept of spirit: this is the case that Derrida makes in the opening pages of *Of Spirit*, where he notes that while a number of related concepts are at stake ("soul or *psyché*, consciousness, *ego*, reason, subject"), it is particularly spirit that Heidegger sets out to avoid. "In order to say what we are, who we are, it appears to be indispensable to *avoid* all the concepts in the subjective or *subjectal* series: in particular, that of spirit" (OS 17–18). Rather than appealing to some notion of spiritual interiority, Heidegger suggests that the entity "we" are (the entity he names *Dasein*) is marked by the power of questioning, is exemplary and privileged for being open to questioning, especially to questioning the meaning of Being.

Through these early chapters of *Of Spirit* (which might well be read alongside his "How To Avoid Speaking: Denials"), Derrida considers Heidegger's strategies of avoidance, particularly his strategies for avoiding spirit, the concept that would only pull *Being and Time* back into metaphysics and cast his existential analysis as a Platonic-Christian theological enterprise. One such strategy of avoidance is Heidegger's placing of quotation marks around "spirit," so that when the word becomes necessary, as it does in his discussion of space and time, it undergoes *Destruktion*, is used in a deconstructed sense, to designate something other than the spirit of metaphysics. When it comes to the "spirit" of *Being and Time*, Derrida suggests, it is as though Heidegger were "citing or borrowing a word he wanted to put to another use" (OS 30), a word through which he wanted to designate a "discourse of the other" (OS 30, 35). Derrida's analysis of this strategy, while brief, is intricate and demanding, particularly if you have not yet studied *Being and Time*. Yet even on first reading, it suggests some of the difficulties Heidegger faces in trying to save "spirit" from the spirit of metaphysics. Derrida suggests that one set of difficulties arises around Heidegger's attempt to "de-Christianize" the spirituality of *Dasein* by thinking of "spirit" as "in time" from the start (as "originary *temporaliza-tion*"), and by thinking of the "fall" as a descent, not from spirit into time, but from one time into another (see OS 27–30).

There is nothing esoteric about Derrida's interest in the role of spirit in Heidegger's text, something that becomes clear when *Of Spirit* moves from *Being and Time* to the *Rectorship Address*, and to the "politics of spirit" (OS 46) that takes shape in the latter text. In the *Rectorship Address*, Derrida points out, although it was delivered only six years after *Being and Time*, Heidegger not only drops the quotation marks around spirit, but even affirms it, "celebrates spirit" (OS 31). The occasion for this celebration of spirit is Heidegger's installation as Rector of the University of Freiburg in 1933, at the time when the National Socialist party under Adolf Hitler is seizing control of Germany and of the German universities. Foregrounding the word "spiritual" (*geistig*)—a word that, Derrida notes, Heidegger will dismiss twenty years later as caught in Platonic-Christian metaphysical thought—the *Rectorship Address* (translated in 1985 as *The Self-Assertion of the German University*) acclaims the "spiritual mission" of the German university and, directly linked to this, Derrida says, it "spiritualizes National Socialism" (OS 39). How, in a mere six years, does Heidegger get from the "discourse of the other" that is suggested by the suspension of "spirit" in *Being and Time* "to the eloquent fervor and the sometimes rather righteous proclamation dedicated to the self-affirmation of the German university? What is the leap from one to the other" (OS 32)?

In his reading of the *Rectorship Address* in *Of Spirit*, Derrida poses, rather than answers, these and other large questions pertaining to Heidegger's "politics of spirit" and its reliance on, and supposed rejection of, a metaphysical and theological heritage. In these pages, Derrida also begins to build the case that spirit is what knots together the four threads that he is tracking in Heidegger's work. Whereas in *Being and Time*, Heidegger describes *Dasein* as an entity distinguished by questioning, in the *Rectorship Address*, Derrida notes, he portrays this questioning as a manifestation of spirit and of will, of a peculiarly German "will to essence" that accords with the "essence of Being" (OS 35–36). Having called attention to this knotting between two of the four threads (the privileging of questioning and of essence), Derrida moves quickly in *Of Spirit* to a text published two years after the *Rectorship Address*, in which, again by means of spirit, a third thread is woven into the knot. In his *Introduction to Metaphysics* (published in German in 1935), Heidegger states that, "The world is always a *spiritual* world." Derrida cites this sentence and notes that in it, Heidegger italicizes *spiritual* (*geistig*), a word first avoided, then hemmed in under quotation marks, "now swelling, exclaimed, acclaimed, magnified" (OS 47). Derrida also notes that in the *Introduction to Metaphysics*, immediately after the sentence, "The world is always a *spiritual* world," Heidegger adds: "animals have no world, nor do they have a world-environment" (see OS 47). If the animal has no world, Derrida interjects, the inevitable consequence is that "the animal has no spirit, as we have just read, every world is spiritual. Animality is not *of spirit*" (OS 47).

With this tying of the question of the animal into the knot of Heidegger's discourse of spirit, Derrida's *Of Spirit* takes its place alongside a number of texts he devoted to the problem of animality in Heidegger's work. Three of these texts, published under the title "*Geschlecht*" are discussed in the *Key Texts* entry following this one. Together with Derrida's additional publications on the animal question, the *Geschlecht* papers and *Of Spirit* comprise what is probably the most extensive and challenging body of work to have come out in recent years on animality in the Western tradition. In *Of Spirit*, reading Heidegger's *Introduction to Metaphysics* as well as his *Fundamental Concepts of Metaphysics* (published in German in 1929), Derrida reveals Heidegger's discourse on the animal to be essentializing and phonocentric. Derrida explains how, for Heidegger in the *Fundamental Concepts of Metaphysics*, animal *benumbedness* is what makes for its absolute difference from the human *Dasein*. Heidegger's animal is not "attuned" to the essence of things. To lack spirit is to lack speech, Der-

> "It is always a matter of marking an absolute limit between the living creature and the human *Dasein*." (OS 54)

rida argues: the benumbed animal cannot question what kind of entity it is, cannot properly question the being of things. While the animal "can use things, even instrumentalize them," it cannot question the essence of technology either, "cannot gain access to a *tekhnè*" (OS 56–57). At this point in *Of Spirit*, Derrida suggests that three of his "guiding threads lace together in this knot: the *question*, the *animal*, *technology*" (OS 57).

By the time *Of Spirit* moves to the fourth and final thread Derrida says is woven into this Heideggerian knot, it is clear that the book takes serious issue with Heidegger's attempt to step outside of a Platonic or Christian metaphysics. This is just what the poet Georg Trakl has done, Heidegger suggests in *On The Way To Language* (published in German in 1953). According to Heidegger, Derrida points out, Trakl's poetry moves beyond the Platonic-Christian epoch, has "crossed the limit" of that tradition, including its very notion of epochality (OS 86). By way of making this case, Heidegger sets up a dialogue between himself and Trakl, between thinker and poet, a dialogue "*on the subject of spirit*," Derrida notes (OS 83). Distinguishing, for example, between Trakl's use of the word spiritual (*geistlich*) and the sense of the word spiritual (*geistig*) that belongs to traditional Christianity, Heidegger attempts to "de-Christianize" Trakl and to remove his poetic work from metaphysics, an effort upon which Derrida casts doubt, even charging Heidegger at one point with resorting to a "massive and crudely typecast form of the metaphysico-Platonic tradition" (OS 95).

That said, Derrida considers *On The Way To Language* to be "one of Heidegger's richest texts: subtle, overdetermined, more untranslatable than ever" (OS 86). It is in his discussion of this text that Derrida reflects on "the promise *of spirit*" (OS 94), the promise that, John Sallis writes, would be the "promise of language itself, as what precedes the question and thus limits its privilege" (Sallis 2008, 65). To reflect further on this "promise" in Derrida's work requires, on our part too, the "fitting patience" (OS 87) that he resolves to bring to his ongoing reading of Heidegger. In *Of Spirit*, Derrida's reading concludes with an imaginary scene, a conversation, between Heidegger and some Christian theologians. At stake in this conversation is what we have been calling, too simply, an indeterminate "third." In the words of Paola Marrati, "what is at stake in the impossibility of 'deciding' upon what is beyond or behind 'metaphysics' is also the possibility of other voices, other addresses" (Marrati 2005, 141).

Geschlecht

In *Of Spirit*, Derrida refers to Geschlecht as a "frighteningly polysemic and practically untranslatable word" (OS 7). The word, untranslated, appears in the title of three of Derrida's published readings of the work of Martin

Heidegger: these comprise *Geschlecht* I, *Geschlecht* II, and *Geschlecht* IV, each of which we will discuss briefly here, specifically in relation to the question of "the animal." *Of Spirit: Heidegger and the Question* belongs between *Geschlecht* II and *Geschlecht* IV. Although Derrida distributed some typescript pages of *Geschlecht* III to a 1985 colloquium, no version of this *Geschlecht* was published before his death. We will consider only I, II, and IV, then, also mentioning some other of Derrida's works that deal with animality, *animal life*, a sustained concern for him, and one that he did not attempt, in binary fashion, to separate off from a thinking of life in general, a *rethinking of life*. For although, as he puts it in his second *Geschlecht*, "no word, no word for word will suffice to translate this word that gathers in its idiomatic value stock, race, family, species, genus/gender, generation, sex" (GII 183), *Geschlecht*, with all its multiple meanings, inevitably touches on the matter of life. The *Geschlecht* publications thus contribute to the "history of life" Derrida alludes to in *Of Grammatology*, a "history" that, not simply anthropocentric, would be "larger" than man (OG 84). Derrida's writings on the animal approach a thinking of life that is not based either in an anthropocentric man/animal hierarchy, or in that hierarchy's reversal into naturalism or biologism. At stake in these papers is something that would be not either dualism or vitalism, some "undecidable" third possibility. Like the "*triton genos*" that Derrida reads in Plato's *khôra* (see Chapter 3 *Key Terms*), it would be some "third genus" *Geschlecht*.

The *Geschlecht* papers arose out of a number of seminars on "Philosophical Nationality and Nationalism" that Derrida gave in the 1980s in Paris. He mentions this at the opening of *Geschlecht* II, where he notes that in the work of the German philosopher Johann Gottlieb Fichte (1762–1814), the word *Geschlecht* has racial and national connotations. This may be one reason why Derrida does not translate *Geschlecht*, so as not to occlude any of the significations the word embeds, even ties together, multifarious meanings that, for instance, can make a discourse on sexuality also a thinking of species difference, and that can make a discourse on species difference into a national and racial politics. This is what happens in Heidegger, whose work is of prime concern to Derrida in the *Geschlecht* publications. What, Derrida asks, is the role of this untranslatable word in the texts of Heidegger?

In asking this question, in all of its complexity, Derrida's *Geschlecht* papers serve as an indicator of what is involved in probing tradition on the question of animal difference, on the legacy of the man/animal opposition, where this one binary leads to so many others. Inextricably linked in the Western tradition to at least as many sites of difference as are laced into the word *Geschlecht*, the question of "the animal" does not stand alone.

Derrida was among the first to recognize this, that animality

> represents the limit upon which all the great questions are formed and
> determined, as well as all the concepts that attempt to delimit what is 'prop-
> er to man,' the essence and future of humanity, ethics, politics, law, 'human
> rights,' 'crimes against humanity,' 'genocide,' etc. (FWT 63)

Students interested in any of these "great questions" should approach
Derrida's *Geschlecht* studies as key texts. Derrida is particularly critical of
Heidegger on the animal question, but we should note at the outset that
his interest is not in proving Heidegger wrong, so much as in learning how
to read and inherit his texts.

Geschlecht I

Derrida's first *Geschlecht* publication, which appeared in 1983, bearing no
number, is titled, "*Geschlecht*: sexual difference, ontological difference."
In this text, Derrida looks into what he calls "the margins" of *Being and
Time*, into the lecture course on logic that Heidegger delivered in 1928
at the University of Marburg/Lahn (translated in 1984 as *The Metaphysical Foundations of Logic*). Here, only one year after *Being and Time*,
Heidegger struggles to write about a topic on which that book is silent: the
sexuality of *Dasein*. In the Marburg course, Derrida points out in *Geschlecht* I, Heidegger underlines the *neutrality* of *Dasein*, explaining that he
chose the term *Dasein* in *Being and Time* precisely for its neutrality. Derrida quotes Heidegger on this point: "For the being which constitutes the
theme of this analytic, the title 'man' (*Mensch*) has not been chosen, but
the neutral title, '*das Dasein*'" (GI 69). *Dasein* does not designate either
a man or a woman. We have a clue here what Heidegger attempts in the
Marburg course, and that is, by way of neutrality, to remove the sexuality
of *Dasein*, at least its *originary* sexuality, from the either/or, man/woman,
binary opposition in which sexual difference is invariably caught. By virtue
of its neutrality, *Dasein* is marked, at the outset, by asexuality, Heidegger
says, using the word *Geschlechtlosigkeit* to refer to this primary sexless-
ness. Derrida is careful to note that this asexuality (*Geschlechtlosigkeit*)
does not, according to Heidegger, de-sexualize *Dasein*. On the contrary, "here one must think of a pre-differential, rather a pre-dual sexuality"
(GI 72), a sexuality that is not yet caught in the snare of a dual opposition.
To think of a sexuality that is already divided—primordially "*dis*-seminated"
but non-dual, marked by "*dis*-persal" but not by binary difference (see GI
75)—would seem to have real implications for ethics, religion, anthropology, psychology, zoology, and other ontic fields of inquiry, but Heidegger
leaves discussion of such things to others, concerning himself in the Mar-

"The 'transcendental dispersion' (as Heidegger still names it) thus belongs to the essence of *Dasein* in its neutrality." (GI 78)

burg course only with the thinking of a "sexual difference that would not
yet be sexual duality" (GI 82). He does not discuss what the original pre-
dual sexuality of *Dasein* implies for understanding the difference between
human and animal life, for the man/animal binary that is as trenchant and
violent as the man/woman opposition of two sexes. Making note of this in
Geschlecht I, Derrida reminds us that Heidegger's analysis of the originary asexuality of *Dasein* is not a philosophy of life, and it "does not deal
with the existent itself" (GI 73). It deals with something older, or younger,
than a worldview, a philosophy, or an ethics, something anterior to any
such determination.

What Heidegger imagines at the origin is not either duality or unity,
but "dispersing multiplicity." He suggests that "originary dissemination"
belongs already to the Being of *Dasein*, that dissemination is an "originary
structure affecting *Dasein* with the body" (GI 75). It is with this Heideggerian point of departure that Derrida's first *Geschlecht* paper primarily
deals. Even before he moves to *Geschlecht* II, and to the duality and dissension into which *Dasein* falls, Derrida's first *Geschlecht* opens to the
"possibility" of a thought of (sexual) difference that would not be "sealed
by a two" (GI 83).

Geschlecht II

Derrida's second *Geschlecht*, delivered at a 1985 conference on
"Deconstruction and Philosophy: The Texts of Jacques Derrida," and
then published in 1987 in a collection of the conference papers, is titled
"*Geschlecht* II: Heidegger's Hand." Derrida says at the outset that this
Geschlecht presupposes familiarity the "brief and modest essay" (GII 161)
that is *Geschlecht* I. While the focus of the first essay is the pre-dual sexuality that Heidegger in 1928 calls *Geschlechtlosigkeit*, the second paper
deals with a *Geschlecht* that is marked by dissension, that is, as Derrida
puts it in closing *Geschlecht* I, "typed by *opposition* or by duality" (GI 83).
What befalls *Geschlecht* as its decomposition, Derrida points out with reference to Heidegger's reading of the poet Georg Trakl, "is a *second blow*
that comes to strike the sexual difference and to transform it into dissension, war, savage opposition" (GII 193). This corruption of *Dasein*'s being
or essence unleashes even "bestial" opposition, Heidegger says, in an
account that he insists has nothing to do with the traditional narrative of

a fall, but that, Derrida notes, borrows nonetheless from both the content and the language of Platonism and Christianity (GII 193). Derrida's analysis in *Geschlecht* II deals not only with this corruption or "decomposition" of *Geschlecht* into animal-like savagery and bestial duality, but also with the prospect that Heidegger poses of the *gathering* of a *Geschlecht*, a race or species or sex, its gathering back or toward essential Being.

Geschlecht II explores both of these motifs, decomposition and gathering, through what Heidegger has to say on "the hand" which, in *Being and Time* and later texts, is a prominent theme in Heidegger's work. Derrida notes, for example, that in *What Is Called Thinking?* (*Was heisst Denken?* 1952), the hand is what differentiates the human from the animal *Geschlecht*. The hand is what *divides*, for as Heidegger contends, only man has the hand; no animal has one. Moreover, there is no equivalency, for Heidegger, between the hand and a paw, claw, or talon, since the hand's being is not as a bodily organ of grasping. The hand *gives* rather than takes, and for this reason, it points to the being who speaks (GII 174–176). The hand both gathers (toward the being who speaks) and divides (the human *Dasein* from the animal). Similarly, as Derrida notes, Heidegger's meditation on "the man of the hand" differentiates the man of the hand (the craftsman, the poet, the thinker) from the mere mechanic, scientist or technician, whose hand is oriented by utilitarian pursuits. Through his *Handwerk*, the man of the hand gathers close to the "as such" of things, close to the essence of *Dasein* as *being-there* (*Da* = there + *sein* = being) to the world in a questioning way (GII 170–171).

Overall, in Heidegger's problematic discourse on the hand, binary oppositions prevail. Moving closely to *What Is Called Thinking?*, *Parmenides*, and other texts, Derrida's reading of this discourse on the hand demonstrates how Heidegger reconstitutes duality, how he sets up an "abyssal"—thoroughly traditional, phonocentric, binary, oppositional—difference between man and animal; and how, in turn, the dichotomy between two species and between two sexes is also a thinking of technology, one that distances the man of the hand from the man of technology whose activities belong to the overall "degradation of the word [speech] by the machine" (GII 179).

In Heidegger's discourse on the hand, it seems that where difference is not "sealed by a two," it is gathered toward the unity of essence. Does Heidegger gesture toward a thinking of *Geschlecht* that would not either divide into duality or gather into one? In the interests of this question, Derrida's second *Geschlecht*, in many ways an unfinished paper, offers the

> "The abyss is speech and thought." Only a being that can speak (think) has the hand: "the hand holds on to speaking." (GII 174)

promise, and even the outline, of a *Geschlecht* III, where Derrida would continue to follow Heidegger's reading of Trakl, and would further probe the nature of what Heidegger calls Trakl's "gathering site" (the contents of the unfinished *Geschlecht* III are summarized in Krell 2006). Is this gathering site single, Derrida asks, "one single site"? Is it "univocal," a "unity of place" (GII 194)? Without *Geschlecht* III, these questions remain "suspended." We will move quickly here to a note on *Geschlecht* IV, where again it is a *third* possibility—in this case, not a third hand but a third ear—that interests Derrida.

Geschlecht IV

Like *Geschlecht* II, Derrida's fourth *Geschlecht* was first presented at a conference, a 1989 event held in celebration of the hundreth anniversary of Heidegger's birth. Published in 1993 in a book collection of the conference papers, Derrida's text is titled, "Heidegger's Ear: Philopolemology (*Geschlecht* IV)." The text is prompted by a brief passage on the voice and hearing from Section 34 of *Being and Time*, "Indeed, hearing constitutes the primary and authentic way in which *Dasein* is open for its ownmost potentiality-for-Being—as in hearing the voice of the friend whom every *Dasein* carries with it" (Heidegger 1962, 206). Beginning with this passage from *Being and Time*, taken with its "furtive and enigmatic brevity" (GIV 166), Derrida's fourth *Geschlecht* charts the "politics of friendship" that emerges from a number of Heidegger's texts, asking what these texts say about the voice of the friend and about the ear with which to hear it. Derrida's intricate reading suggests that where, in Heidegger, a hierarchical opposition determines the difference between hearing and not-hearing, between having and not-having a friend, the problematic of the animal returns with a vengeance, the animal that is "world poor," and that, Derrida notes, has neither language nor the experience of death; the animal that has no hand, that has no friend, and that has no ear either (GIV 172). Set within a discourse on the animal, the ear, like the hand, either divides or gathers to unity, to the essence of things. *And yet*, Derrida suggests, there is more than one ear, and there are not just two ears, in Heidegger. This is the suggestion with which *Geschlecht* IV leaves us: that the voice of the friend might reach us only through a third "ear of the other" (see also GII 196, n. 38).

"It is really a matter of the voice of the other." (GIV 175)

> "For so long now it is as if the cat had been recalling itself and recalling that, recalling me and reminding me of this awful tale of Genesis, without breathing a word. Who was born first, before the names?" (AT 387)

Other Animal Essays

Additional to the *Geschlecht* papers, a number of Derrida's texts take up the animal question. We conclude this entry with passing reference to some of these. The Chapter 3 *Key Terms* entry on phonocentrism (and on carno-phallogocentrism) mentions "'Eating Well,' or the Calculation of the Subject" (1991), an interview in which Derrida considers the issue of sacrifice, the "sacrificial structure" of Western discourse in general, and the need to "sacrifice sacrifice" in coming to terms with animality. The essay "Rams" (delivered in 2003 as a memorial to Hans-Georg Gadamer and published in translation in 2005 as a chapter of *Sovereignties in Question*) returns to the hand and to sacrifice, and to the sacrificial animal, the ram. *Aporias* (French publication 1993, English translation also 1993), in a meditation that links death with the foreigner, or the figure of the foreign, examines Heidegger's distinction between dying and perishing, as another border that separates *Dasein* (who dies, and is open to his own proper dying) from the animal (who can only perish). Finally, we must mention two of Derrida's studies, both published in English as full-length essays on the animal, both originally part of an extended presentation he gave at the 1997 Cerisy-la-Salle conference on his work, "L'Animal Autogiographique." Among other things, both of these English translations, "The Animal That Therefore I Am (More to Follow)," and "And Say the Animal Responded?," open the question of animal response, and the Cartesian distinction (that is made also by Jacques Lacan) between response and reaction, this too as an indivisible border between human and animal.

> "Lacan holds that the animal could not itself have an unconscious, an unconscious of its own." (AS 123)

Given Time / The Gift of Death

The thought of the gift, already broached by Derrida in a number of texts, including *Geschlecht* II, is explored at length in *Given Time* (published in French in 1991, translated in 1992) and in *The Gift of Death* (published in French in 1992, translated in 1995).

Both texts are of major importance to students of religion. In them, Derrida draws on a range of texts—including the Hebrew Bible and New Testament, writings of the Czech philosopher Jan Patocka, and works by Sören

Kierkegaard, Marcel Mauss, Emile Benveniste, Claude Lévi-Strauss, Heidegger, Charles Baudelaire, and Emmanuel Levinas—to consider such questions as what constitutes a religion; the human/animal division implied by the traditional distinction between religion and cult; sacrifice; the family; links between religion and economic rationality in the Western tradition; the gift and giving as distinguished from economic reasoning, from an economy of return and exchange; death as gift; and, as in the animal essays, what tradition bequeaths us on the notions of moral and ethical responsibility.

The gift is another instance of what Derrida calls "the impossible" (see Chapter 3 *Key Terms*), in that, as he puts it in "On the Gift," his exchange with Jean-Luc Marion, "it is impossible for the gift to appear as such" (OTG 59). There is such a thing as a gift, but only as "the experience of this impossibility" (OTG 59). This means that as soon as a gift is identified as such, "then it is canceled as a gift. It is reintroduced into the circle of an exchange and destroyed as a gift. As soon as the donee knows it is a gift, he already thanks the donator, and cancels the gift." By the same token, Derrida says, "[a]s soon as the donator is conscious of giving, he himself thanks himself and again cancels the gift by re-inscribing it into a circle, an economic circle" (OTG 59). The gift is not amenable to ontology or phenomenology. There is no "as such" of the gift. The gift is not even amenable to naming. Indeed, with the gift, as with God, it is "the name of the name" that finds itself put into question (GT 10). "The gift is totally foreign to the horizon of economy, ontology, knowledge, constative statements, and theoretical determination and judgment" (OTG 59). Yet, as Derrida notes, this impossibility of the gift did not prevent him from writing books on it, and it does not preclude giving. As he writes in *Given Time*: "if the gift is another name of the impossible, we still think it, we name it, we desire it. We intend it" (GT 29).

The Gift of Death and *Given Time* are two of Derrida's attempts to think the gift. The first part of *Given Time* proceeds as a detailed analysis of *The Gift*, written by the French sociologist Marcel Mauss (1872–1950), a text that, Derrida says, in its reliance on economy and exchange, "speaks of everything but the gift" (GT 24). By way of developing his theory of the gift as "another name of the impossible" (GT 29), Derrida in *Given Time* also reads, in conjunction with Mauss' *The Gift*, a short story by Charles Baudelaire, "Counterfeit Money," in *The Gift of Death*, Derrida attempts to show that it is the "economy" of the gift, "the economic axiomatic"

"I am interested in Christianity and in the gift in the Christian sense." (OTG 57)

(OTG 59), that works in certain Christian texts, including Jan Patocka's *Heretical Essays on the History of Philosophy*. At the same time, Derrida attempts to open this economy to what is not exhausted by a phenomenological or theological determination. Working from within Christian texts (for example, Kierkegaard's *Fear and Trembling*), but working against any association of the gift with the economy of a return-to-self, Derrida tries to think the possibility of the impossibility of the gift.

Memoirs of the Blind

This book, the full title of which is *Memoirs of the Blind: The Self-Portrait and Other Ruins*, is a 1993 translation of a 1990 French text (*Mémoires d'aveugle: l'autoportrait et autres ruines*) that was published in conjunction with an exhibition of the same title held at the Louvre Museum in Paris between 26 October 1990 and 21 January 1991. The exhibition was organized by Derrida on the invitation of the Louvre curators, as the first in a series of exhibitions to be put together, largely from the Louvre collection, by well-known thinkers who were non-specialists in the domain of art. The Louvre curators gave the series the title *Parti Pris*, or "Taking Sides," and they promised full—even "sovereign"—authority to the guest curators to choose the theme, and works to be included, in each exhibition (see "Translators' Preface," MB vii). No doubt, an invitation to participate in the *Parti Pris* series came as a challenge to the guest curators—Derrida said he was both honored and intimidated by the invitation that was extended to him (MB 36). The series was also intended to challenge art historians and specialists, to whom it would provide an opportunity to look beyond their field, to see art from other perspectives, and to have their own sight enriched by what the organizers called "another *gaze*" (qtd. in "Translators' Preface," MB vii).

It might seem surprising that, asked to open onlookers' eyes to other ways of seeing, Derrida chose blindness as the theme for his exhibition. To some extent, the theme is self-referential. For example, Derrida writes in the book of the way that art "blinds" him, exposes his ignorance about how to look and what to see (MB 36). He was, he says, aware of his artistic incompetence from early childhood, and it set him apart from his older brother, a talented draftsman, whose drawings were on display in every room of the family house (MB 36–37). *Memoirs of the Blind* is replete with such autobiographical details as these. It includes dream accounts; descriptions of a facial paralysis that all-but blinded Derrida during the period when organization of the exhibition was underway; recollections of Derrida's father burying the dead in his community in Algiers; meditations on Eli and Elijah, "which turns out to be one of my first names" (MB 23); accounts of Derrida writing without seeing—on a notepad beside his bed in the night, or a scrap of paper while he is driving a car. Not incidentally, *Memoirs of the Blind* was written at the same time as "Circumfession," another experiment in autobiographical writing. It complicates the autobiographical status of these two texts that both are written as polylogues, a structure of interlaced voices in which it is difficult, even for Derrida, to decide who is speaking (EF 29–30; see also the discussion of "Circumfession" in Chapter 5 below). Both works are rich in religious motifs, and both deal with a number of the same themes, including inheritance, family, writing, faith, testament, memory, death, and mourning. In "Circumfession," Derrida explores these themes by way of reading *The Confessions* of Saint Augustine (354–430), the Christian Church Father who, like Derrida, was born in north Africa. In *Memoirs of the Blind*, it is primarily to biblical blind men that Derrida turns.

This is a beautiful book. As the translators Pascale-Anne Brault and Michael Naas point out, it is not simply an exhibition catalogue, for the text that accompanied the works shown at the Louvre was not the same as that found in the book, and while the exhibition displayed forty-four drawings and paintings, seventy-one images are included in the book ("Translators' Preface," MB viii). The images are of drawings and paintings of blindness, of the blind, mostly blind men, "blind *men*, notice, since the illustrious blind of our culture are almost always men," Derrida writes just a few pages into the book, "as if women perhaps saw to it never to risk their sight" (MB 5). The question of inheritance is already at stake in this observation, the question of how to read, how to look at, the sexual difference encoded in these "great paradigmatic narratives of blindness" that are "dominated by the filiation father/son" (MB 5–6 n.1). A few of the narratives are Greek, but most of them are biblical, particularly Hebrew Bible narratives, such as the stories of Issac and Jacob, Tobias and the angel, Tobias healing his father's blindness, Cain and Abel, and Jacob's dream. There are some New Testament stories here too: the book includes several depictions of Christ healing the blind and of the blinding conversion of Saint Paul. Many of the works are taken from the canon of "great art" (Caravaggio's *The Conversion of Saint Paul*, Coypel's *Study of the Blind*, Rembrandt's *Jacob's Dream*), though works by many lesser-known artists are also included. We might add that not only Old and New Testament stories are at issue in *Memoirs of the Blind*, but also the relationship between the two testaments—which one sees with too natural, too exterior, or too carnal an eye—and even the status of "testament" and of the "testamentary" (MB 20–23).

> "And faith, in the moment proper to it, is blind." (MB 30)

This book is not, as the translators point out, an exhibition catalogue. Neither is it, despite its autobiographical dimensions, "the journal of an exhibition" (MB 36). Derrida makes this point more than once, also suggesting, however, that he considers the exhibition portraits to be *self-portraits*. This is his "first hypothesis" in the book: that drawing (writing, painting) "is blind" (MB 2); that "one writes without seeing" (MB 3). *Memoirs of the Blind* is an extended meditation on this hypothesis, on the senses in which, from the outset, at the "origin," drawing (writing, painting) is blind. Derrida notes, for example, that in the instant when one turns to the page or the canvas and begins to trace in pencil or paint, one no longer holds the model (object, idea) in sight: from the beginning, then, the trace (*trait*) belongs, not to perception, but to memory, thus to an "unconscious" that can never be made fully present. *Memoirs of the Blind* replaces the immediacy of perception with such memory, "*memory of the trait*" (MB 3), and in so doing, it not only thwarts the "return-to-self" referentiality of self-portraiture and of autobiography, but also counters "the whole history" of Western philosophy that privileges knowing (the *idea*, *eidos*, *idein*), and that ties knowledge to sight (MB 12). According to Derrida's notion of the *trait*, one writes from the memory of what has always already withdrawn. Writing (drawing, painting) is thus *structurally* in the dark, which puts us all in the position of Butades, the Corinthian lover whose story "relates the origin of graphic representations to the absence or invisibility of the model" (MB 49). Joseph-Benoit Suvée's painting, *Butades or the Origin of Drawing*, serves as a good illustration of Derrida's "second hypothesis" in this book: "a drawing of the *blind* is a drawing *of* the blind" (MB 2), a drawing *of* the act of drawing in the dark.

Memoirs of the Blind is a good companion text to read alongside "Faith and Knowledge," written just a few years later and discussed in the next entry, for both works deal with an archaic "faith," a kind of "reflecting faith," that is *blind*, completely heterogeneous to knowledge (the sight of knowledge *blinds* one to this faith), and that cannot be appropriated by any religious tradition. "And faith, in the moment proper to it, is blind," Derrida writes in his discussion of the *Book of Tobit*. In this Deuterocanonical text, the elder Tobit is blinded by bird dung after burying one of his own people. When his sight is restored by his son Tobias who, acting on instructions from the angel Raphael, rubs fish gall in his father's eyes, Tobit *gives thanks*, Derrida points out. It is as if what is restored to Tobit is the vision of a "law beyond sight" (MB 29). In Derrida's way of looking at paintings and drawings of the Tobit story (by Rembrandt, Pietro Bianchi, and after Rubens), the artists are concerned more with "*observing* the law beyond sight" (MB 29) than with "representational fidelity" (30) to the details of the

Book of Tobit. "What guides the graphic point, the quill, pencil, or scalpel is the respectful *observance* of a commandment, the acknowledgement before knowledge, the gratitude of the receiving before seeing, the blessing before the knowing" (MB 29–30). What the artists depict, Derrida suggests, is the "debt or gift" (MB 30) at the origin of painting or drawing.

In giving thanks, Tobit sees (receives) the hand of the other that promises the blind man sight. Not only in the Tobit story, Derrida notes, but in these narratives overall, "the *mise en scène* of the blind is always inscribed in a theatre or theory of the hands" (MB 26). His analyses of this theory of the hands make *Memoirs of the Blind* also a good companion text to *Of Spirit* and the "*Geschlecht*" papers, as well as to *On Touching —Jean-Luc Nancy* ("As with touching, the laying on of hands orients the drawing. One must always recall the other hand or the hand of the other" [MB 9]). *Memoirs of the Blind* should also be read in conjunction with *The Work of Mourning*, for, as in the *Book of Tobit*, the exhibition paintings and drawings are stories of mourning, in which "tears or veiled eyes" (MB 24) preclude clear sight. Finally, *Memoirs of the Blind* is a crucial text for Derrida's understanding of *witnessing* as blind—as, like writing (drawing, painting), not a matter of perception so much as of memory.

Faith and Knowledge

This paper is written as fifty-two aphorisms. Derrida used the aphoristic, "telegraphic," form more than once so as to compose a series out of multiple entries that need not confirm, and might well contradict, each other. This disjunctive form enacts repetition with difference, and so is a good match for his work. The form serves Derrida well in "Faith and Knowledge," where he does not offer a conclusive response to the question, "what of religion today?" so much as outline a number of points on which the question calls for further reflection and research. Insofar as it figures something machine-like in the dissociated elements it puts out, the aphoristic form is appropriate to Derrida's argument in "Faith and Knowledge" that analyses of religion cannot separate it from, or oppose it to, the mechanistic, to science, technology or tele-technoscientific reason. Even when it wars against these powers, religion today allies itself with telecommunications and technoscience, Derrida maintains:

> it produces, weds, exploits the capital and knowledge of the tele-mediatization; neither the trips and global spectacularizing of the Pope, nor the interstate dimensions of the "Rushdie affair," nor planetary terrorism would otherwise be possible. (FK 82)

The aphoristic form is not incidental or ornamental, then, but crucial to Derrida's argument in "Faith and Knowledge" that religion is "autoimmune," that when it wars itself against the forces of modern technoscience, religion is attacking what already lives within its own body (see the Chapter 3 *Key Terms* entry on "autoimmunity"). As a final comment on the aphoristic form, we might recall aphorism 45 from Derrida's "Fifty-two Aphorisms for a Foreword," a (1989) text on architecture, "There is always more than one aphorism" (FA 69), another indicator of the form's suitability for "Faith and Knowledge," where, among other things, Derrida puts "religion in the *singular*" into question (FK 64).

Derrida delivered "Faith and Knowledge" on 28 February 1994 on the Isle of Capri at a philosophical forum organized on a topic that he suggested: "religion," the contemporary "return of religions." It was Derrida who suggested that the forum might address the question (to be posed "in an areligious, or even irreligious manner") of "what religion at present might *be*, as well as what is *said* and *done*, what *is happening* at this very moment, in the world, in history, *in its name*" (FK 61). As it turned out, and as Derrida notes in his paper, the philosophers who actually gathered around the table on the Isle of Capri, himself included, were not particularly well-positioned to address the topic, "religions" in the *plural*—the "religions" of the "return of religions" conference theme. For those who assembled at the Capri forum represented but four different languages, and only European languages at that (German, Spanish, French, Italian). No Muslim was among them, Derrida notes; no delegate from other cults either, and not a single woman (FK 45). The delegates shared a "common culture," manifestly Christian, "barely even Judaeo-Christian" (FK 45). What, then, prepared the members of this "fraternity" to address the conference theme *without* privileging a single religion, Christianity, or at best, Judaeo-Christianity? Derrida's paper raises this question, addressing it specifically to the Capri conference participants, but also giving it a wider scope: "When we speak, *we Europeans*, so ordinarily and so confusedly today about a 'return of the religious,' what do we thereby name? To what do we refer?" (FK 69).

The significance of Immanuel Kant for Derrida's paper is already suggested by the paper's full title: "Faith and Knowledge: The Two Sources of 'Religion' at the Limits of Reason Alone," which comes close to repeating the title of Kant's 1793 book, *Religion Within the Limits of Reason Alone*. Yet, with its quotation marks around the word, "religion," Derrida's title inscribes a suspension (*epoché*) of certainty around the word that Kant's

> "No faith, therefore, nor future without everything technical, automatic, machine-like supposed by iterability. In this sense, the technical is the possibility of faith, indeed its very chance." (FK 83)

book presumes to define. And as another point of difference, where Kant's title delimits religion to the domain of reason, puts religion *within* the limits of rational mastery, Derrida's title locates "religion" (in quotation marks) *at* the limits of reason, where efforts at rational mastery and totalizing synthesis fail. For Kant, as Derrida points out in his paper, there are only two families of religion: the religion of cult and the religion of reason (see also, *The Gift of Death*). The latter, rational religion, concerns itself solely with morality, not with disputed matters of biblical or theological interpreta- *awhad* tion, which are inessential to it. Rational religion subordinates knowledge *int* to what Kant defines as "reflecting faith," which is not dependent on historical revelation and which is opposed to all forms of dogma. For Kant, "reflecting faith" is essentially Christian, and of all the positive religions, only Christianity approximates pure morality.

After examining Kant's thesis, Derrida remarks that it "seems strong, simple, and dizzying: the Christian religion would be the only truly 'moral' religion; a mission would thus be reserved exclusively for it and for it alone: that of liberating a 'reflecting faith'" (FK 50). Kant's thesis assigns an evangelical mission to Christian "reflecting faith," a point that Derrida relates to what he calls contemporary "globalatinization," the situation of a global political rhetoric (largely an American rhetoric) that is articulated through an essentially Christian (Latin, Roman) "evangelical" and political discourse on religion. This discourse opposes the ideals of Christian morality and rationality—and democracy—to the so-called forces of evil—to "fanaticism," "terrorism," and "fundamentalism," all of which are usually tied to Islam.

Derrida notes in "Faith and Knowledge" that those who assembled at Capri were not "men of faith," theologians or priests, but philosophers, "men of reason." And yet, in what constitutes a crucial moment in his paper, Derrida suggests that it is to *faith* that these "men of reason" might give their attention. Consider Kant's notion of "reflecting faith," Derrida says to the Capri participants, for it is "a concept whose possibility might well open the space of our discussion" (FK 49). With this suggestion, to be sure, Derrida does not endorse Kant's privileging of rational religion, or of Christianity as *the* religion of reason. Derrida does not endorse or espouse *any* determinate religion, least of all one with a global imperial mission. But neither does he wave Kant away. Rather, Derrida asks what might be made of Kant's *separation of faith from knowledge*, and he proposes of this Kantian separation that "[e]ven today, albeit provisionally, it could help us structure a problematic" (FK 49).

The word "structure" is important here, as it always is for Derrida. Taking his departure from Kant's concept of a faith that is independent of historical revelation and of the dogma of any determinate religion—working as well from Heidegger's positing of a "revealability" that is *more originary* than revelation—Derrida attempts to describe a transcendental "structure of experience," an experience of faith, that would be universal, but that "would *precede* all determinable community, all positive religion, every onto-anthropo-theological horizon. Like Plato's *khôra*, as Derrida reads the term against Plato, Kant's "reflecting faith," as Derrida reads the term against Kant, would link pure singularities *prior* to any social or political determination, *prior* to all intersubjectivity, *prior* even to the opposition between the sacred (or the holy) and the profane" (FK 55, emphasis mine). The *originary* "structure of experience" that Derrida struggles here to describe is characterized by *interruption* and *opening*—and we might think of a number of other related words, such as *spacing, tearing, breaching, rift, incision, wound, crypt,* even *writing* (see the above entry on *Geschlecht I*).

To understand more of what Derrida means by this structure that belongs to the experience of faith, it is necessary to read slowly through a number of his works, for this transcendental structure is an *aporia* to which he turns again and again, always as a matter of how to inherit tradition and of how to respond, affirmatively, to a traditional text such as Kant's *Religion Within the Limits of Reason Alone*. It seems that every time Derrida returns to this issue of this structure, he adds another, differential, element to his discussion, so much so that we cannot presume, on the basis of a single text like "Faith and Knowledge," to glimpse the whole picture. One text at a time, and "Faith and Knowledge" is a good place to begin, particularly by reading carefully through those sections of the paper in which Derrida elaborates on the *messianic* and *khôra*. These two "names" that Derrida takes from tradition become "figures" ("differentials") for the "originary structure" in question, a structure that is, like the gift, impossible to name.   'd. Hévenc' ?

Derrida's "Faith and Knowledge" is one of his most important treatments of religion, and of why and how he distinguishes between "religion" and "faith," between the privileging of a single religion or culture and the "universalizable culture of singularities" (FK 56) to which, he thinks, *khôra* and the messianic lead. Derrida's paper is couched in a meditation on the traditional and religious themes of *island, Promised Land,* and *desert*. The paper is a key source for his concept of "life." It provides a significant introduction to his analysis of "democracy," and a fundamental introduction to his concept of "autoimmunity."

Rogues

First published in France in 2003 under the title *Voyous* and comprising two major lectures Derrida delivered the previous year—in the months following 9/11 and prior to the American invasion of Iraq—*Rogues* (translated 2005) examines two essentially irreconcilable principles, that of *democracy* and that of *sovereignty.* In the course of examining these two principles, Derrida analyses the concept of "autoimmunity" that he considers in "Faith and Knowledge" and in the interview "Autoimmunity: Real and Symbolic Suicides," in *Philosophy in a Time of Terror*). *Rogues* is important for students of religion not only for reason of its development of this concept of the autoimmune, but also because it probes what Derrida considers to be the Christian theological heritage of the problematic concept, the "phantasm," of sovereignty. *Rogues* is also a crucial source for Derrida's thinking of justice and of what he calls "democracy to come."

By way of illustrating what claims to sovereignty entail, *Rogues* opens with *The Wolf and the Lamb*, the famous fable by Jean de la Fontaine that tells the story of a wolf who, on the lookout for prey, happens upon a young lamb drinking in a brook, then immediately accuses the lamb of muddying his water. Four accusations are leveled against the lamb, who has the chance to protest his innocence in regard to only three of the charges before the wolf drags him into the woods and eats him—thus making the case that "might is right," or that, as la Fontaine puts it in the first line of his fable, "The strong are always best at proving they're right" (R x). In this fable, Derrida suggests, the wolf represents *sovereign* force, the force that makes, and lays down, its own law, that declares what is right, and that gives itself the right to do so. The sovereign, the one claiming such rights, including the right to use force, could be an individual or it could be a political entity such as a nation-state (an entity that is unthinkable apart from sovereignty). In either case, sovereignty is characterized by *ipseity*, by arrogating to oneself, to the one-self (*ipse*), "the power that *gives itself* its own law" (R 11). Through this *ipsocentric* positioning of oneself as both cause and end, sovereignty charts a kind of circularity, an economy of return. It "is round," Derrida says, for it turns on and around the one who claims mastery, inscribing the "return to self, toward the self and upon the self" (R 10) of a circle. In Chapter 3, we discuss this circular rotation upon the self as the *auto-affection* that belongs to *phonocentrism* and to the ideal interiority it ascribes to *hearing-oneself-speak*. As is evident from his Husserl studies and from the three books he published in 1967, Derrida's scholarly work really begins with the deconstruction of this auto-affectivity and of the phonocentric privilege that, he says, prevails throughout the tradition of metaphysics. It can thus be said that, even in an early work such as *Speech and Phenomena*, Derrida's analysis was already deconstructive of the politics of sovereignty. *Rogues* continues the deconstruction, chiefly with reference to democracy, which is the locus of sovereignty that really interests Derrida in this book.

It is difficult to imagine a democracy that would be without ipseity, that would not grant a certain sovereignty to the self, to the so-called autonomous subject (*autos, ipse*) who is the claimant of the freedoms we call individual rights. Yet in declaring that freedom belongs equally to all, in espousing freedom *and* equality, democracy is fundamentally at odds with itself. It betrays an "internal contradiction," an "undecidability" (R 35), between the autonomy of its free and self-determining subject, and the heteronomy that opens freedom equally to all, not only to the strongest, but to minorities, the poor, the weakest of the weak. Democracy works by calculation, by counting votes and establishing criteria for citizenship, while at the same time embracing an idea of *equality in freedom* that can have nothing to do with numerical calculations or determinations of worth. Throughout *Rogues*, whether he is reading a canonical text on democracy by Aristotle or a contemporary work such as Jean-Luc Nancy's *The Experience of Freedom*, Derrida contends with this "undecidability" within democracy, which, as he puts it, "risks paralyzing and thus calls for the event of the interruptive decision" (R 35). Democracy embodies two laws, Derrida explains in the first chapter of *Rogues*. It represents "the return to self of the circle and the sphere, and thus the ipseity of the One, the *autos* of autonomy, symmetry, homogeneity, the same, the like, the semblable or the similar, and even, finally, God," and in tension with this, democracy holds to another truth, "another truth of the democratic, namely, the truth of the other, heterogeneity, the heteronomic and the dissymmetric, disseminal multiplicity, the anonymous 'anyone,' the 'no matter who,' the indeterminate 'each one'" (R 14–15). It is in part for reason of this internal contradiction that, Derrida says, while we are heirs of democracy, we do not yet know what the Greek word means, "what it assigns to us, enjoins us, bequeaths or leaves us" (R 9).

In the course of discussing this contradiction within democracy, Derrida returns to the concept of "autoimmunity," the "autoimmune law," that he considers at some length in "Faith and Knowledge." The two irreconcilable principles that Derrida examines in *Rogues*— sovereignty vs. democracy, the law of ipseity (*autos, ipse*) vs. the law of heteronomy—provide him with rich material for a discussion of autoimmunity, a discussion that is never far-removed from faith and knowledge, religion and science, or religion and culture concerns. For example, by citing the political philosopher Alexis de

> "As always, these two principles, democracy and sovereignty, are at the same time, but also by turns, inseparable and in contradiction with one another." (R 100)

Tocqueville from his 1835 treatise, *Democracy in America*, Derrida makes the point that the concept of sovereignty has a theological origin. Tocqueville's book celebrates nineteenth century America as *the* achievement of the democratic idea, for reason that the American people —in perfect circularity, Derrida notes, working by *itself and for itself*—rule over the political world as God reigns over the universe (R 13–14). For Tocqueville, God is the model of the unbroken, indivisible, sovereignty that America has translated into political terms. Derrida draws out this biblical, primarily Christian, theological heritage of sovereignty in *Rogues*, arguing that the concept of sovereignty belongs to "a long cycle of political theology that is at once paternalistic and patriarchal, and thus masculine, in the filiation father-son-brother" (R 17). It is this "barely secularized theology" (WA 207) that gets taken into democracy, where divine sovereignty underpins the idea of the indivisible "sovereignty of the people" (R 17). In the course of analyzing this politicized theology, Derrida makes the point that sovereignty is, of necessity, autoimmune. Like religion, sovereignty cannot remain integral, intact, unscathed, indivisible or pure. The entity claiming sovereignty bears within itself the heteronomy, the "foreignness," against which it would close off and autoimmunize itself, even to the point of paralysis or death.

Derrida's analysis of the theological heritage of sovereignty, of sovereignty's autoimmunity, of sovereignty's place in democracy: these have a particularly American focus in *Rogues* where, he says, "democracy and America" is his real theme (R 14). For one thing, this focus helps us to appreciate autoimmunity as indispensable to the ethical and political analysis Derrida offers in *Rogues*, particularly of a post-Cold War and post 9/11 world, where threats to democracy come "from within," and where the autoimmune response to threat is evident. Unlike Tocqueville, who heralded American society as the realization of "the idea" of democracy as unbroken sovereignty, Derrida holds that heteronomy is the condition of any justifiable exercise of power (his discussion of the democratic principles that operate in the United Nations, as distinct from the unjustifiable sovereignty exercised by superpowers in the Security Council, is significant here), and that the "idea" of democracy, freedom alike for all, while unrealizable, impossible, is an unconditional demand. Although "incalculable equality in a freedom that is alike for all" (R 49) has not been realized by any existing democracy, and will never exist in the present, it remains the unconditional and the "impossible" promise of "democracy-to-come."

Chapter 5

Derrida's religion

Questions for J.D.

During the roundtable discussion, "*Confessions* and 'Circumfession'," that took place at Villanova University in September 2001 at the conference "Religion and Postmodernism 3: Confessions," Richard Kearney, on behalf of John Caputo, asks Derrida a pointed question. Referring to Derrida's remark in "Circumfession" that "I quite rightly pass for an atheist" (Cf 155), Kearney asks: "why don't you simply say, 'I am an atheist'?" (CC 38). Derrida answers that he does not know. "If I knew, I would say that I'm an atheist or I'm not, but I don't know." Derrida then adds another important statement to his response: "I don't know for the reasons that I've been trying to explore for years and years. It depends on what the name God names" (CC 38).

In one respect, Kearney's question seems odd and out of place. For it is not usually considered appropriate to ask a speaker at an academic

---

The chapter at a glance:

In Derrida's work, religion and autobiography are often related, both as sites of *undecidability*.

- This chapter considers some instances where Derrida broaches the topic of religion autobiographically.
- The chapter attempts to leave undecidability in play, and makes no attempt to resolve issues of Derrida's religious affiliation or belief.
- In order to let Derrida speak for himself, the chapter proceeds by way of outlining his answers to some questions he was asked about "his" religion.

---

conference a question pertaining to his or her personal beliefs. Indeed, whether a speaker is or is not an atheist is currently regarded as irrelevant to a discussion of scholarly work, perhaps especially where the academic study of religion is concerned. And yet, as we mention in the next chapter, Derrida's "passing for an atheist" has been remarked on several times and raised as a curiosity at each of the Villanova "religion and postmodernism" conferences organized to assess the importance of his work for the study of religion. Granted, Kearney's question is posed during a roundtable discussion of the text, "Circumfession," in which Derrida makes the "passing for an atheist" remark. As well, the question comes at a conference that explores links between Derrida's "Circumfession" and Augustine's *Confessions*, both "autobiographical" texts. But as we mention in the Chapter 4 *Key Texts* entry on *Memoirs of the Blind*, another of Derrida's "autobiographical" works, the "I" in "Circumfession," the "I" in the "I quite rightly pass as an atheist" remark, cannot be read in a naively referential way. Or so Derrida tells us himself, when he says of "Circumfession" in particular that it is a complex multi-voiced text, in which the narrative "I" is impossible to pin down, and in which Derrida is "not making a confession. I am not signing a confession. I am not speaking in my own name" (EF 29).

Still, we cannot dismiss Kearney's question. Indeed, Derrida's response suggests that, somehow, the question, and his own incapacity to answer it directly, touches an "undecidability" at the very heart of his work. Religion is an important site, though not the sole or privileged site, for Derrida's exploration of this undecidability. So is autobiography. This chapter brings these two together, religion and autobiography, since the two are so often joined in Derrida's work, albeit with a good deal of undeciability in play. So as not to resolve this undeciability in favor of some determination of Derrida's religious affiliation or belief, the chapter tries to let Derrida speak for himself. The chapter, very briefly, provides some of Derrida's answers to questions he was asked about the matter of "his religion."

If he prayed

Derrida, by his own account, was someone who prayed every day—*if* he prayed. He did not speak of his praying, the prayers he performed daily, without introducing the undecidability of an "if": *if I pray, when I pray*. For prayer, as he understood it, has nothing to do with knowledge or truth. Indeed, for prayer to happen, all certainty must be suspended, and expectation of answer or calculation of benefit must be given up. Of course, as Derrida acknowledged, the child who prays expects answers, but for the adult, prayer cannot belong to an economy of return. Might prayer, then, like the gift—offered to an unknowable other and without any expectation

Confessing his prayer

In "Epoché and Faith: An Interview with Jacques Derrida," John D. Caputo asks Derrida:

> "If you rightly pass for an atheist, to whom are you praying? How would your prayers be answered? Who do you expect to answer these prayers?" (EF 28)

of benefit to oneself—be another experience of the "impossible"? Perhaps so, for "when one prays one is always a child" (EF 30).

Speaking of his own prayers in the interview "Epoché and Faith," Derrida refers to their "childish" layer, which would include images from the Judaism of his youth, "images of God as a Father—a severe, just Father with a beard—and also, at the same time, images of a Mother who thinks I am innocent, who is ready to forgive me" (EF 30). Added to this, another layer

> involves my culture, my philosophical experience, my experience of a critique of religion that goes from Feuerbach to Nietzsche. This is the experience of the nonbeliever, someone who is constantly suspicious of the child, someone who asks, "To whom am I praying?" (EF 30)

This is the layer where certainty is suspended—the *epoché* ("suspension") of the interview title—and for Derrida at least, it is a layer *inclusive* of all experience: "all the texts I've read, from Plato to Saint Augustine to Heidegger, are there. They are my world, the world in which my prayers are prayed" (EF 31).

If Derrida prayed, this is the way that he prayed. And he prayed every day. We have to say *if*, since, as Derrida reminds us, we cannot judge another's prayers. Nor can we know them, which is another aspect of prayer's "suspension." Although one often prays in a public setting such as a synagogue, and partakes in ritual gestures and in a tradition's common language, there remains an element to prayer "that is absolutely singular and secret—idiomatic, untranslatable" (EF 30). In this sense, even when Derrida prayed aloud and in public, his prayers were silent and private. So he explains in the "Epoché and Faith" interview: "That is the way I pray, *if* I pray. And I pray all the time, even now" (EF 30).

The last of the Jews

Although Derrida never denied, or attempted to hide his Jewish descent, and always felt honored to claim it (AO 6), he was uneasy for many reasons about calling himself "a Jew," about what he termed the "impossible utterance," "I am Jewish," or "I am a Jew" (ATG 42). For one thing, he said he did not know what the statement, "I am a Jew" means or what it

---

An impossible utterance

In the "Confessions and 'Circumfession'" roundtable discussion, Hent de Vries puts this to Derrida:

> "My question relates to another important motif in 'Circumfession' that I would like to ask you to comment on a little bit more, namely, the formulation, 'I am the last of the Jews. I am the last of the eschatologists'." (CC 36).

---

names: is it a declaration of authenticity, one that presumes the distinction between authentic Jew / inauthentic Jew? Who can say who or what is an authentic Jew? "Who can speak in the name of Judaism?" (ATG 41). Once again, Derrida called here for a suspension (*epoché*) of certainty, for undecidability as to what constitutes authentic Jewish identity, or as to what about "jewishness" or "being-jew" (*judéité*) is authentic or inauthentic. In "Abraham, the Other," the paper he delivered to a December 2000 colloquium on the topic of his relationship to Judaism, Derrida suggests that this undeciability between the authentic and the inauthentic, "this aporetic experience of undecidability or of the impossible" (AO 51), is essential and "the very condition, in truth, the milieu or the ether within which decision, and any responsibility worthy of the name (and perhaps worthy of the name and of the attribute *jew*) must breathe" (AO 31).

In part, Derrida's "retreat" from the appellation, "I am a Jew," stemmed from a sense of his own insufficiency or inadequacy to declare himself "a Jew" when "I don't know Hebrew, or hardly any: I am very unfamiliar with Jewish history or the texts of Jewish culture" (ATG 43). Keenly aware, from his early days in Algeria, of this "lack of culture in relation to Judaism" (ATG 43), Derrida said more than once, "I am the last of the Jews" (Cf 190; ATG 42). In an interview with Elisabeth Weber, Derrida explains that the statement has several meanings. One of these clearly is, "I am the least of the Jews"—lacking as a Jew, the last Jew to deserve to be called a Jew (ATG 42). This is the sentiment Derrida expresses in "Abraham, the Other," where he admits to feeling flustered, worried, and intimidated by the prospect of a conference given to the topic of his relationship to Judaism. On the conference title, *judeities* ("being-jewish"), Derrida explains, "I feel, and will always feel, out of place in speaking of it; out of place, misplaced, decentered, very far from what could resemble the thing itself" (AO 4).

In the same paper, "Abraham, the Other," Derrida relates his "retreat" from the appellation, "I am a Jew," to a "caution against community" (AO 15) that was already developing in him by the age of ten. Derrida explains this caution by way of recalling "how the word *jew*" first reached him, how and when in his childhood he first encountered the word. He did not initially hear it in his family, but at school in El Biar, where the word *jew* (which inevitably implied "dirty Jew") reached him, he says, "like a blow, a denunciation, a de-legitimation prior to any right, prior to any legality" (AO 10). Derrida speaks of this blow as something he had to carry for the rest of his life, as if the word were "a weapon or a projectile that has sunk into your body, once and for all and without the possibility of every uprooting it. It adheres to your body and pulls it toward itself from within, as would a fishing hook or a harpoon lodged inside you, by way of the cutting and wet edge, the body of each of its letters, *j.e.w.*" (AO 11). Aside then, from the enormous question of how one so wounded by it might now "speak honorably of this word *jew*" (AO 11), Derrida's experience of anti-Semitism in Algeria prompted him to withdraw from all discourses of belonging and not-belonging. As he explains this in "Abraham, the Other":

> my suffering as a persecuted young Jew (common enough, after all, and not comparable to those endured in Europe—something that adds to all the reserve and decency that prevent me from speaking of it), this suffering has no doubt killed in me an elementary confidence in any community, in any fusional gregariousness, whatever its nature, and beginning of course with any anti-Semitic herding that alleges ethnic, religious, or national roots and of which my trained vigilance knows how to recognize the signs and decipher the symptoms. (AO 15)

We can learn from *Rogues* how, for Derrida, a "life" and a "work" intertwine; how Derrida's early caution with respect to community became in time a carefully reasoned critique of "the very value of the ensemble, of *Versammeln*" (R 11), of whatever is gathered together on the basis of sameness, resemblance, similarity, and simultaneity; and of whatever, in that gesture of gathering, bounds off dissimulation or difference. Speaking of the history and philosophy of democracy in *Rogues*, Derrida asks whether or why one must live together only with one's like, which is also the question of how a community—whether a fraternity, a family, or a nation-state—contends with the heterogeneous and the dissymmetric. Thus, while Derrida's distrust of community was born, we might say, of his anti-Semitic experience (he said of the anti-Semitic system that it was the first corpus he learned to deconstruct), the critique that grew out of this youthful caution was directed more widely to all communal gathering based on likeness, including the community that was his own.

Here is another sense in which Derrida refers to himself as "the last of the Jews": he is critical of Judaism's discourse of *exemplarism*, even more so of its claim to *election* or *chosenness*. What Derrida calls *exemplarism* "would consist in acknowledging, or claiming to identify, in what one calls the Jew the exemplary figure of a universal structure of the living human"

(AO 12). The "more jewish the Jew," Derrida says, the more he would represent this universal structure, this "universality of human responsibility for man, and the more he would have to respond to it, to answer for it" (AO 12). This figure of exemplarity is what makes it possible for some to say, "I am Jewish" in a way that testifies to universality (see ATG 41). The doctrine of *election* makes it possible for some Jews to say, "We are the chosen people," that is, "not only God's allies, God's chosen, but God's witnesses, and so on" (ATG 41). Unable to embrace discourses of exemplarity, election, or messianism, Derrida still calls himself "the last of the eschatologists" (Cf 75). On the one hand, he says in attempt to explain this, he is obsessed by eschatology, by death, mortality, the last (CC 37). On the other hand, he is the worst Jew, "the last one, really" (CC 37). This is the "existential aporia" in which he and his work remain caught. Derrida adds that the aporia is precisely "the condition for responsibility, the condition for a decision, the condition for addressing the other" (CC 38).

The Judaeo-German couple

For all Derrida's "silence" on the appellation, "I am a Jew," a silence that he understood in an almost religious sense (AO 7), the Jewish question, in one way or another, is always present in his work. In many cases, such as *Glas* and its analysis of "the Jew" in Hegel and Kant, or in texts devoted to such thinkers as Hermann Cohen, Franz Rosenzweig, Walter Benjamin, and Gershom Scholem, the "Judeo-German psyche" (see ATG 45–46) is something that Derrida examines and tries to understand. He refers to the Judeo-German couple as "terrifying" (ATG 46), a "knot" bound up by the complex question of the German Jew's fascination with the German, and the German's fascination with the Jew. Derrida said that the knot needs to be unraveled, that is, studied and thought through (ATG 47).

For Hegel, as Derrida demonstrates in *Glas*, the Jew is "absolutely foreign, infinitely foreign" (ATG 46), an element excluded from philosophy, from family, from German culture, and so on. Yet, as Derrida also points out in *Glas*, the excluded element can also be the woman (for Hegel, the sister), just as it can be the non-European. In short, Derrida says, "it is all figures of the other," one of which can become exemplary. "The Jew can be an exemplary figure" of the excluded other, figure of "a crypt excluded

---

An unavoidable and impossible alliance
In *Questioning Judaism*, Elisabeth Weber asks Derrida this question:

"What is it that always makes you come back again to the unavoidable and impossible alliance, to the Judaeo-German psyche?" (ATG 45).

---

non-exemplarity of Jew comp other others — women etc.
/ —substitution, etc.

on the inside" (ATG 48). The Jew, then, might be an exemplary figure of
what Derrida calls the autoimmune.

We should note that Derrida responds to Elisabeth Weber's question
("What is it that always makes you come back again to the unavoidable
and impossible alliance, to the Judaeo-German psyche?") autobiographically. "I am not simply Jewish, certainly, but I am Jewish," he says, "and
although I'm not German, I was raised in a culture and a philosophical tradition for which the German inheritance is inescapable" (ATG 45). Somehow, the undecidable "I" of Derrida's response embodies both a Jewish
and a German heritage. Perhaps, then, it is no wonder that, as Weber
suggests, we are in Derrida's texts "constantly being sent back and forth
between the 'German' side and the 'Jewish' side, to the point that we can't
really distinguish them precisely from each other" (ATG 45). Again, it is the
"specular" link between these two in the texts of some Jewish and German thinkers, the fascination that becomes especially "knotted up" under
Nazism, and even during the period of Nietzsche and Wagner: it is the
history of this knot that, Derrida says, needs to be unraveled, one nodal
point at a time (ATG 47).

Circumcision

Interviewing Derrida in "A Testimony Given…" (in *Questioning Judaism*),
Elisabeth Weber remarks that from *Glas* to "Circumfession," by way of
The Post Card and "Shibboleth" (in *Sovereignties in Question*), Derrida's
work comprises a meditation on circumcision (ATG 39). We could add
other texts to the list of those in which Derrida "turns around" the figure of
circumcision, and we could then ask, with him, "What does *figure* mean
here?" (PT 341).

As Derrida explains, circumcision refers, among other things, to "a certain mark that, coming from others and submitted to in absolute passivity,
remains on the body, visible and no doubt indissociable from the proper
name which is likewise received from the other" (PT 341). On the basis
of this explanation alone, we can appreciate that the circumcision around
which a text like "Circumfession" turns is both "fact and figure" (see Capu-

> **Under the name of circumcision**
> In "A 'Madness' Must Watch Over Thinking" (in *Points…Interviews
> 1974–1994*), Derrida notes that every time there is a mark or a name
> received from an other, the *figure* of circumcision imposes itself on him.
> He then asks (himself) this question:
>> "What does 'figure' mean here?" (PT 341)

Handwritten margin notes:
- N (X) circumcision (problematised by exemplarity) + other 'rings' as universal, simply have, concept of limit = concept of concepts that is itself unlimited.
- ie as one figure of the rings, limit or cut.
- from?

to 1997, 233). As "fact," we might say, the circumcision of "Circumfession" refers to an actual procedure, at once medical and religious, the peritomy that was performed on the infant Jacques ("Jackie") Derrida in 1930, at the same time that the Hebrew name Elijah was conferred upon him—Elijah being "the most 'eschatological' and thus the most awaited of the prophets" and the one appointed by God to preside over each circumcision (Cf 82). The entrance of Elijah on the scene might suggest that our description of circumcision is no longer just a matter of fact, and that even with respect to the medico-religious procedure, circumcision already exceeds the factual plane. It is interesting and perhaps related to this point that, since the image of Elijah that is printed in the Bennington-Derrida book occupies a full page (81), we cannot say for certain whether it belongs to the upper text, the expository discourse of Geoffrey Bennington's *Derridabase*, or to the lower text, the more figurative prose of Derrida's "Circumfession." Even the illustration of the medical instruments used in circumcision (in 1723 in Amsterdam), taking up all of page 67, blurs the boundary that would separate the calculable from the aleatory: tools for a surgical incision from figure of a wound.

The ritual cut of circumcision left on Derrida's body an "indestructible mark" (PT 341) of membership in the Jewish community. Insofar as this mark of an "ineffaceable alliance" (PT 341) translates into a logic of exemplarity, it represents a problem, a "problem of figure" (ATG 40), with which Derrida struggles in his work, the difficult experience of his "relationship to... I don't venture to say Judaism—let's say to circumcision" (ATG 40). This experience was as painful and as permanent as any scission made in his skin. Thus, paradoxically, for Derrida, the "bad Jew" (ATG 42), who did not circumcise his own sons (Cf 221), circumcision is an incessant concern. "Circumcision: that's all I've ever talked about, consider the discourse on the limit, margins, marks, marches, etc., the closure, the ring (alliance and gift), the sacrifice, the writing of the body, the *pharmakos* excluded or cut off" (Cf 70).

Derrida suggests to Elisabeth Weber in "A Testimony Given..." that, possibly for reason of his "ignorance" of Jewish culture and sense of dislocation from it, he began to consider circumcision as something that happens in all cultures, as universal: "on the one hand the singular alliance of the Jewish people with their God, but just as well, on the other hand, it could figure a sort of universal mark that we find not only in men but also in women" (ATG 40). In this regard, Derrida might be thinking *through* psychoanalysis, and, as was the case all along (consider what he says about the trace and the *grammè* in *Of Grammatology*), he might be thinking of the body (and of life) as always already written. As he explains to Elisabeth Weber:

> The poetical relationship to language is the experience of what makes us born into language, to language's already-being-there, to the fact that language precedes us, governs our thought, gives us the names of things, etc. This poetical experience of language is from the outset an experience of circumcision (cutting and belonging, originary entrance into the space of law, non-symmetrical alliance between the finite and the infinite). And so, in quotation marks and with all the necessary rhetorical precautions, a "Jewish experience" (ATG 43).

According to Derrida, we can only receive this "universal circumcision" (ATG 43) as "a gift" come from the other. As such, as both a gift and an opening to the other, circumcision figures what cannot be appropriated by one self: "the impossibility of recovering, of recovering oneself, of coming back to oneself, that's what it is, the openness of the gift" (ATG 44). Circumcision comes from the other—prior to memory and before the self/other, same/different, either/or boundary—such that, for the one who inherits the gift, everything begins with response; with what Derrida called "an originary 'yes'" (AO 3). In this sense, as John Caputo suggests with reference to "Shibboleth" and "Ulysses Grammophone," circumcision, for Derrida, is "the cut that breaks the bonds of the self-enclosure of the same and makes possible the in-coming of the other" (Caputo 1997, 262).

Obsession with the name

When Geoffrey Bennington asks him whether there is some continuity across his work in its characterizations of God, Derrida answers affirmatively. There is some continuity, and more than that, "some continuity in the obsession with the name, with the names, of God" (CC 34).

To demonstrate this obsession would require consideration of many texts. Derrida mentions "How to Avoid Speaking: Denials" (see the Chapter 3 *Key Terms* entries on *differance* and *trace*) as but one of these texts. We might want to add "Abraham, the Other," where, as in the story of Abraham called by God to sacrifice his son Issac, "everything begins for us with the response," everything begins with the "yes" that is implied in all responses (AO 3). Can we then think of the "originary 'yes'" (AO 3)

Geoffrey Bennington, during the "*Confessions* and 'Circumfession'" roundtable, asks Derrida a question about God:

"whether you think that, across your work, the name 'God,' or the concept of God, or the treatment of that concept, has changed." (CC 34)

---

of deconstruction as a response to God? Derrida answers this question in "How to Avoid Speaking," where he distances his work from negative theology or from any discourse that leads back to the Christian deity, to a Supreme Being, or to any determination of what the name God names. Deconstruction does not respond to any omnipotent being, not Christianity's God and not the nameless God of Abrahamic traditions. Derrida's interests are more along the line of deconstructing theologically-based notions of sovereignty (EF 37), what he calls the "onto-theological-politics of sovereignty," in favor of "some unconditionality that would not be sovereign," and that "might be associated, not with power, but with weakness, with powerlessness" (CC 41; see also the Chapter 4 *Key Texts* entry on *Rogues*).

And yet, Derrida prayed, *if* he prayed, every day. He did so without assigning any certainty to the side of the addressee. The uncertainty of the addressee, part of the structure of the trace, extends absolutely to God, to this name. "God would be the name of the absolutely unknown indeterminate addressee" (CC 35).

(neg theol ?
there is no absolute)

A prophetic postscript

When, in a 1984 interview with Richard Kearney, "Deconstruction and the Other," he is asked whether his work is prophetic, Derrida is undecided in his response. On the one hand, Derrida "concedes" that the style of his questioning "as an exodus and dissemination in the desert might produce certain prophetic resonances" (DO 119). These are the resonances that John Caputo, in *Prayers and Tears*, suggests "are the very substance of [Derrida's] Jewishness" (Caputo 1997, 230). "It is possible to see deconstruction as being produced in a space where the prophets are not far away," Derrida goes on to say to Kearney. "Perhaps my search is a twentieth century brand of prophecy." But on the other hand, "it is difficult for me to believe it" (DO 119).

> **Richard Kearney asks Derrida:**
>
> "Do you feel that your own work is prophetic in its attempt to deconstruct philosophy and philosophical criteria?" (DO 119)

Chapter 6

Derrida and religion

Entering the field

It is impossible to deny the enormous significance that Derrida's work has, and has had, for the study of religion. But his writing did not gain an immediate reading or reception within the field. In *Jacques Derrida*, Geoffrey Bennington comments on the resolute blocking suffered in France after 1967 by Derrida's work, and by those associated with it, "the doors of the university definitively closed" (Bennington 1993, 331). Attempts to block Derrida occurred outside of France as well, for example at Cambridge University in Britain in 1992, when a proposal by the institution to grant Derrida an honorary degree occasioned an international controversy (see Derrida's discussion of this in "*Honoris Causa*: 'This is *also* extremely funny'" in PT 399–421). North American universities were also wary of Derrida's work, which entered the academic institution, not through phi-

---

The chapter at a glance:

The purpose of this chapter is to sketch Derrida's contributions to the field of the academic study of religion.

The sketch is necessarily selective.

It is divided into a number of sections, the titles of which help to organize a vast body of material in brief and outline form.

Section titles are not hard-and-fast, and in some cases, work discussed in one section might just as well be placed in another.

While other sections might be added and further contributions considered, the chapter should give you a good sense of why, for students and scholars of religion, Derrida is a key thinker.

---

losophy or religion departments, but through literature and comparative literature units. During the 1970s and 1980s while Derrida's texts were becoming increasingly available in English translation, the North American study of religion was caught up in its own transition, from a theologically-based Christian (barely Judaeo-Christian) enterprise, to a world religions endeavor concerned to distinguish the academic study of traditions from confessional approaches. As a result of this change, profession of belief in the dogmas of a given tradition was no longer considered a prerequisite for students or scholars of religion. Though ready dismissals of Derrida are still common across the disciplines, often by academics who have not read him—who, as Derrida once put it, "like bad journalists, [repeat] stereotypes without reading the text" (DN 8–9)—the climate in religion is now more conducive to serious study of his work. It remains the case, however, that as late as 2001, John D. Caputo was still commenting on the oddity of having Derrida speak at a conference on religion, when Derrida says of himself in "Circumfession" that he "quite rightly passes as an atheist" (Cf 155; see also Caputo, Dooley, and Scanlon 2001, 1; see also Caputo and Scanlon 1999, 1–2).

John D. Caputo is an astute reader of Derrida, also a central figure in mediating Derrida's work to the field of religion. Caputo suggests that Derrida felt himself out of place among religionists, for he was not a trained theologian or biblical scholar, and was "intimidated" (Derrida's word) by the prospect of speaking to a gathering of such specialists (see Caputo, Dooley, and Scanlon 2001, 1). It is good to remember, as if Derrida would let us forget, that he was not a theologian or biblical scholar, and that he did not approach the question of "religion" from within the profession of any determinate faith. It is also important to remember just how much he spoke and wrote about religion, a point that Gil Anidjar makes in his Introduction to *Acts of Religion*. By way of commenting on how much the study of religion has already benefited from Derrida's work, and how the recognition of his importance for the field is growing, Anidjar lists over thirty of Derrida's texts in which the question of religion is at issue (see Anidjar's "Introduction," AR 2). — *Q here of rel'n of relig + metaphysics*

What makes Derrida a Key Thinker for the study of religion, however, turns not just on what he said or wrote about religion. As is evident from the diverse ways it is informing and transforming the discipline, his work overall is significant for religionists. Hans-Georg Gadamer suggests as much in the paper he presented at the 1994 colloquium on the Isle of Capri (Gadamer 1996, 200–211), where he notes that the question of religion leads inevitably through Derrida to Plato, Marx, Hegel, Heidegger and others on whom he worked. It is impossible to limit Derrida's relevance for

well yes

religion only to texts that deal specifically with the topic. At least for scholars of religion, it seems impossible to limit his relevance to Western traditions: Harold G. Coward's publications on Derrida and Indian philosophy (1990) and Derrida and Bhartrhari (1991) are but two examples from a burgeoning area of comparative research.

Religion and postmodernism

The term "postmodernism" is not one that Derrida adopted. Indeed, he consistently put all such homogenizing *–isms* into question, this one in particular, given its periodizing implications (postmodernism as the epoch that follows the modern), and given the apocalypticism that proliferated around the term (postmodernism as the collapse of the modern that Fredric Jameson describes in 1984 in "Postmodernism, or the Cultural Logic of Late Capitalism," or the moral decline that Alasdair MacIntyre portrays in 1981 in *After Virtue*). And yet, despite his refusal of it, Derrida's texts were tagged with the "postmodern" label, and often enough, they were made a ready example of the ills his critics wanted to decry with the term. It is fair to say that much of the initial reception of Derrida's work within the field of religion was under the "postmodern" banner, in part through the *Religion and Postmodernism* conferences organized by John Caputo and his colleagues at Villanova University. In the case of these conferences, however, Caputo suggests playfully, the word "postmodernism" was used not to define Derrida's work but just "to draw a crowd" (Caputo, Dooley, and Scanlon 2001, 1; see also Caputo and Scanlon 1999, 1–2). Each of the Villanova conferences centered on questions Derrida's work raises for the study of religion. Each involved participation from Derrida, and each resulted in a "Derrida and religion" volume. Individually and together, these volumes provide one good overview of Derrida's impact on the field.

The first of these conferences, organized by Caputo and Michael Scanlon and held at Villanova University on 25–27 September 1997, brought scholars together to dialogue with Derrida on the question of religion at the end of the millennium, and in particular, as Caputo and Scanlon point out in their introduction to the conference volume, *God, the Gift, and Postmodernism*, to provide the forum for a face-to-face dialogue between Derrida and the French theologian Jean-Luc Marion on questions of mystical theology and the gift (Caputo and Scanlon 1999, 1). Marion's opening paper examines, and takes some issue with, Derrida's writing on negative theology and its relation to the "metaphysics of presence." Both in his response to Marion (pages 42–47 of *God, the Gift, and Postmodernism*) and in his "On the Gift" discussion with him (pages 54–78), Derrida's response suggests many points of agreement between himself and Marion, also some matters of difference, including the question whether negative theology and the "metaphysics of presence" are actually linked in Derrida's texts. Derrida's response to Marion touches on negation, prayer, and the role of the "third" in his work, and so it would be a good addition to the *Key Texts* we discuss in Chapter 4. *God, the Gift, and Postmodernism* includes an additional dialogue between Derrida and Marion on the gift, and on the Christian sense of this term; in this dialogue, Derrida elaborates further on *khôra* (see Chapter 3, *Key Themes and Terms*) as the "third" that, to that point, he had been trying to read against the Greek and Judaeo-Christian heritage of the gift. The other papers included in this inaugural volume (including contributions from David Tracy, Richard Kearney, Mark Taylor, Edith Wyschogrod, Françoise Meltzer, Scanlon, Caputo and others, along with additional responses from Derrida), indicate that by 1997, Derrida's work had contributed significantly to religion through study of such topics as the gift, spirituality, mysticism, negative theology, feminism, comparative theology, and even historical Jesus research.

The second Villanova *Religion and Postmodernism* conference, held on 14–16 October 1999 and resulting in the book, *Questioning God* (edited by Caputo, Scanlon, and Mark Dooley, published in 2001), centered on two topics: God and forgiveness. Derrida delivered an opening paper to the conference on forgiveness ("To Forgive: The Unforgivable and the Imprescriptible"), and forgiveness was also the subject of roundtable discussion with Derrida and the other speakers, moderated by Richard Kearney. While it carries forward issues raised at the first conference, *Questioning God* moves much more decisively into religions' thinking of forgiveness, as well as into the lead question of God—and of *questioning* God (and the privilege of "questioning" that we discuss in the Chapter 4 *Key Texts* entry on *Of Spirit*). It is evident from the papers included in *Questioning God* that within two years of the first Villanova conference volume, Derrida's impact on the study of religion had grown decisively. Also evident here, and indicative of the picture overall, is the range of areas within the clearly interdisciplinary field of religion in which Derrida's work proves significant. For instance, *Questioning God* includes papers on: ethics and theology, forgiveness and incarnation, memory, faith, narratives of God, questioning God, idols of God, selfhood and the postmodern subject, the rhetorical subject, the Virgin Mary, and radical orthodoxy. Finally, and also typical of Derrida's reception within the field, some papers included in *Questioning God* take sharp issue with his work.

While overshadowed by the events of September 11, 2001, the third Villanova conference, held on 27–29 September 2001, was remarkable in a number of ways, perhaps especially for its philosophical input—and this not only from Derrida in his opening address, "Composing 'Circum-fession'" (CC). As is suggested by the conference volume, *Augustine and Postmodernism: Confessions and Circumfession* (edited by Caputo and Scanlon, published in 2005), Derrida's work by this time had effectively blurred the disciplinary boundaries separating religion from philosophy. A number of the conference participants, philosophers rather than reli-gionists, came together at the 2001 Villanova event to discuss shared religio-philosophical concerns: Geoffrey Bennington, for example, deliv-ered a paper on "Time—for the Truth," Hent de Vries spoke on "Temporal Modes from Augustine to Derrida and Lyotard," Philippe Capelle spoke on "Heidegger: Reader of Augustine," and Catherine Malabou presented a paper on "The Form of an 'I'" (see Caputo and Scanlon 2005). No doubt, it was obvious by 2001 if not long before, that Derrida's significance for the study of religion could not be parceled out from his "philosophical" import, or from his readings of the Western philosophical tradition that traces its beginnings to Plato.

A number of additional "religion and postmodernism" studies have brought Derrida's work into the field, Edith Wyschogrod's *Saints and Post-modernism* as but one example. Mark C. Taylor's explorations, via Der-rida, of what he calls a "postmodern a/theology" (see Taylor 1984) have led, through discussion of oppositional differences in Christian theology (Taylor 1987), to "after God" analyses. Taylor's *Nots* (1993) is one of the latter analyses, a text that, with continuing recourse to both Derrida and theology, broaches the question of ethics in an after-God world.

Messianism and the messianic

Derrida's *Specters of Marx: the State of the Debt, the Work of Mourn-ing, and the New International* (published in French in 1993, translated in 1994) is based on a two-part presentation he gave to a multinational and multidisciplinary conference, "Whither Marxism? Global Crises in Interna-tional Perspective," held at the University of California, Riverside in April 1993. It is not possible here to summarize Derrida's book, which has much to say about: *hauntology*, the "logic" of the specter or the revenant; "end of history" discourse; justice and the gift; the double injunction of inherit-ance; mourning; animality; the political; democracy and the "new interna-tional." *Specters of Marx* is also a critical source for Derrida's thinking of the messianic as a structure of experience that cannot be equated with Jewish messianism or with any type of traditional messianism, religious or secular. Derrida's distinguishing of what he called the messianic or mes-

sianic faith (see the Chapter 4 *Key Texts* entry on "Faith and Knowledge")
from messianism of any stripe led to considerable debate inside and outside the field of religion. This debate is one instance where disciplinary
boundaries are again blurred, much to the chagrin of some of Derrida's
critics. Something of the intensity of this criticism can be glimpsed from
Ghostly Demarcations, a set of response papers to *Specters of Marx*,
edited by Michael Sprinker and published in 1999. As Sprinker notes in his
Introduction, "condemnation predominates" in this volume, and is directed
against Derrida particularly by the Marxist contributors to the book who
cast his work as an abstract French "demarxification" that "depoliticizes"
(see Sprinker 1999, 1–4).

It is important to note how often these contributors refer dismissively
to *Specters of Marx* as an example of "postmodern" writing. In "Marx &
Sons," his response to the contributors published in *Ghostly Demarcations,* Derrida repeats his refusal of the label, comments on the inadequacy of this and other "catch-all" terms (MS 228–229), explains that
he considers himself neither a poststructuralist nor a postmodernist, and
insists that the delimiting of terms (e. g., what is "political"?) is very much at
issue in *Specters of Marx* and in the *Ghostly Demarcations* responses to it.
Derrida is clearly distressed in "Marx & Sons" over the ongoing misreading
of his work (see for example (MS 221–223), his incredulity over Gayatri
Spivak's misreadings and "manipulation" of *Specters of Marx* in her 1995
paper "Ghostwriting"), misreading that certainly impacted on the reception
of his work. It seems clear from the *Specters* debate that Derrida's refusal
of all determinate orthodoxies was unsettling to many scholars, including
religionists, as was the non-utopianism of his messianic faith (for further
reading, see for example, Wise 2001).

The Derrida-Habermas encounter

It seems that Derrida never did shake the "postmodern" label, for as Lasse
Thomassen notes in the Introduction to *The Derrida-Habermas Reader*, in
the long exchange he had with the German philosopher and social thinker
Jürgen Habermas (b.1929), Derrida was cast as representing postmodernism over against Habermas, the great thinker of modernity (Thomassen
2006, 2). The Thomassen collection is valuable, providing a chronology
of the exchange between Derrida and Habermas, a collection of the rel-
evant texts, and a number of scholarly essays on the many (ethical, political, critical) issues at stake in the exchange. The exchange really begins
with the publication in German in 1985 of *The Philosophical Discourse of
Modernity* (translated 1990), in which Habermas attacks Derrida for his

postmodern leveling of the genre distinctions between philosophy and literature, reason and rhetoric (see Habermas 1990; Thomassen 2006, 13–34). Derrida's interview response to these charges, included in the Thomassen volume (pages 35–45), suggests that Habermas has misread him, or has not read him at all. From these fairly bitter beginnings, and despite their obviously very different approaches, Derrida and Habermas went on to develop a respectful discussion on issues of mutual concern, particularly on the future of institutions of international law and challenges facing Europe (HT 303–305), a discussion that was cut short by Derrida's death. This exchange provided another avenue through which Derrida's work entered the study of religion, a field in which, partly for his association with the Frankfurt School of Critical Theory, Habermas has been studied for decades. One important outcome of the Derrida-Habermas encounter is *Philosophy in a Time of Terror. Dialogues with Jürgen Habermas and Jacques Derrida* (2003), in which Giovanna Borradori interviews both thinkers on 9/11 and issues of terrorism and responsibility (the interview "Autoimmunity: Real and Symbolic Suicides," is an important source for Derrida's concept of autoimmunity (discussed in Chapter 3 *Key Terms* and in the Chapter 4 *Key Texts* entry on "Faith and Knowledge"), a concept that has particular pertinence for the study of religion.

Hermeneutics

Much has changed over the past two decades in the way religionists teach and research hermeneutic methodologies. When John Caputo published *Radical Hermeneutics* in 1987, it was possible to put the words "hermeneutics" and "radical" together, something that is more difficult to do today, not she? in part for reason of changes resulting from religionists' study of Derrida's work, and in part for reason of two exchanges Derrida had, one with Paul Ricoeur and the other with Hans-Georg Gadamer, on the question of whether hermeneutics, in its search for meaning, belongs to metaphysics, and is thus irreconcilably at odds with deconstruction. Rather than reviewing the rich literature that contemporary hermeneutics has produced, much of which engages Derrida's work (see for example, Handelman 1982; 1983; Silverman and Ihde 1985; Silverman 1994), we will focus here on Derrida's exchanges with Ricoeur and Gadamer.

During the 1960s, the distinguished French philosopher Paul Ricoeur (1913–2005) began to publish a number of fundamental works on hermeneutics (see for example, in translation, Ricoeur 1976; 1981), one of which, *The Rule of Metaphor* (1977), takes strong issue with Derrida, specifically with Derrida's essay on metaphor, "White Mythology: Metaphor in the Text of Philosophy" (published in *Margins of Philosophy*). Ricoeur introduces

his criticism of Derrida in the process of offering his own theory of metaphor. In this theory, metaphor is a discursive segment (never a single word,
always at least one sentence long) that results in semantic innovation: new
meaning, poetically (metaphorically) generated, and passed from poetry to
philosophy. In a "subversive manoeuvre," Derrida's deconstruction counters this movement, Ricoeur contends, and it thus threatens to destroy
metaphysics (Ricoeur 1977, 287).

Derrida responds to Ricoeur in "The *Retrait* of Metaphor," suggesting,
here too, that he has been misread, and returning to some of the intricacies of his reading of Heidegger in "White Mythology." The debate between
Derrida and Ricoeur is complex. Without trying to summarize all it involves
(for more detail, see for example, Joy 1988), we can note that, in responding to Ricoeur, Derrida suggests an alignment between hermeneutics and
metaphysics. While Ricoeur's positing of a continuist ascent, from poetry
to philosophy, resulting in the assimilation of poetry by philosophy, seems
to be a version of the Hegelian dialectic, Derrida argues, in another vein
altogether, that one cannot produce a philosophical treatise on metaphor
that is not itself treated (infused) with metaphor, thus that philosophy cannot claim to occupy a preserve above and outside of the poetic. Moreover,
Derrida says, texts cannot be interpreted without reference to the *trait* out
of which they are constituted, the *trait* that is structurally in withdrawal
(*retrait*) and never either properly philosophical or merely figural (see the
Chapter 3 *Key Terms* entry on *trace*).

At least in part, the Derrida-Ricoeur debate concerns traditional disciplinary and genre boundaries, particularly the division between literature and
philosophy and the kind of language that befits reason, as distinct from
rhetoric. The same issues are raised by the encounter that Derrida had with
John Searle in the context of speech act theory (see Derrida's LINC). The
issue of genre has also been raised as one specific to religion, for example
in analyses of the relation between autobiography and criticism in "Circumfession," or of the significance of Derrida's "figural" writing on Judaism (see
for example, Robbins 1995; Caputo 1997). Many institutional and political
matters are bound up with so-called "genre leveling," along with problemat-
ics of the signature and "hermeneutic" questions regarding the very nature
of academic work (e.g., the question whether "figurative" is synonymous
with "frivolous," not the stuff of a serious academic discourse).

At first blush, the encounter between Derrida and the German philosopher Hans-Georg Gadamer (1900–2002) appears to suggest, along the
lines of the Derrida-Riceour debate, that the interests of hermeneutics and
deconstruction cannot be reconciled. Gadamer studied under Heidegger
and in 1960 wrote *Truth and Method*, a major treatise in philosophical (dia-

lectical) hermeneutics, still a classic text in the study of religion. Gadamer's encounter with Derrida spanned many years, from a first meeting in Paris in 1981 to Gadamer's death in 2002. The details of the encounter, along with the Derrida and Gadamer texts involved, at least to 1989, are made available in English in *Dialogue & Deconstruction: the Gadamer-Derrida Encounter* (Michelfelder and Palmer 1989). What becomes interesting about this encounter over time are the points in common that gradually develop between these two very different thinkers, and very different readers of Heidegger. Indeed, as early as 1985, Gadamer could say that Derrida's deconstruction "involves something quite similar to what I am doing," in that both he and Derrida endeavor to supersede "any metaphysical realm of meaning" (Gadamer, "*Destruktion* and Deconstruction" in Michelfelder and Palmer 1989, 132). The common ground shared by Gadamer and Derrida is an important subject for study. An essential source for this study is Derrida's "Rams: Uninterrupted Dialogue—Between Two Infinities, the Poem," first delivered as a public lecture in memory of Gadamer at the University of Heidelberg on 5 February 2003, and published in translation in Derrida's *Sovereignties in Question: The Poetics of Paul Celan*.

Ethics, politics, legal and feminist studies

A key "Derrida and religion" text is John Caputo's *The Prayers and Tears of Jacques Derrida*, published in 1997. We have discussed Caputo's crucial role in facilitating "religion and postmodernism" studies of Derrida. While *The Prayers and Tears of Jacques Derrida* might well be viewed as part of that effort, the text also stands apart as a careful and sympathetic exposition of the ethical promise of Derrida's work—the ethical promise of "the impossible." Caputo reads deconstruction as response to a *tout autre* that is un-nameable and forever undecidable, but for him, this undecidability leads not to apathy or impassivity but to "passion" for the impossible, to "desire" for justice (see for example, Caputo 1997, 25–26). *metaphys...* While acknowledging that it belongs not to any determinate religion but to the experience of "faith" and of the "messianic" that Derrida discusses in his Capri paper on "Faith and Knowledge" (see the *Key Texts* entry in Chapter 4), Caputo suggests that Derrida's "passion for the impossible" has distinct Jewish roots. and...

Much scholarly discussion of Derrida's work has evolved around the ethical and political implications of deconstruction's opening to the other as "wholly other," the *tout autre* Caputo refers to in *Prayers and Tears*. Some of this discussion develops as comparative study of deconstruction in relation to the work of Emmanuel Levinas, which is one aspect of Caputo's book, also a subject-area in its own right. For example, Simon Critchley's

The Ethics of Deconstruction: Derrida and Levinas (1992) reads several of Derrida's central motifs in relation to the thinking of ethics in Levinas; John Llewelyn's *Appositions of Jacques Derrida and Emmanuel Levinas* (2002) examines modes of intercrossing between the writings of Derrida and the writings of Levinas, always with a view to ethics, justice, responsibility, and impossibility; and *Re-Reading Levinas*, a collection edited by Robert Bernasconi and Simon Critchley (1991) and including a contribution from Derrida on Levinas' work, centers on ethical responsibility and what the editors call an ethical structure of reading. One section of the latter collection deals with ethics and the feminine, an area that, from early on, has been broached by Derrida-Levinas studies (see for example Dallery and Scott 1989; Grosz 1995), and that has been a significant site for exploration of Derrida's work.

At least where deconstruction is concerned, it is difficult and unnecessary to draw fixed boundaries between "women's studies" and "religious studies" research, as is evident from two important collections of essays on questions of the feminine and feminist ethics in Derrida's work: *Feminist Interpretations of Jacques Derrida*, edited by Nancy Holland in 1997, and *Derrida and Feminism. Reading the Question of Woman*, edited by Ellen Feder, Mary Rawlinson, and Emily Zakin in the same year. The Holland collection features some classic texts in the Derrida-and-feminism field: Christie V. McDonald's 1982 "Choreographies" interview with Derrida, Gayatri Spivak's "Displacement and the Discourse of Woman," Nancy Fraser's "Force of Law: Metaphysical or Political?" and Drucilla Cornell's "Civil Disobedience and Deconstruction." This collection includes additional contributions from Elizabeth Grosz, Peggy Kamuf, Peg Birmingham, Kate Mehuron, Ellen Armour, and Dorothea Olkowski. The collection brings together Derrida-and-religion (e.g. Armour's contribution) and Derrida-and-feminism studies. The Feder volume does so as well, reprinting Jane Gallop's "'Women' in *Spurs* and Nineties Feminism," alongside contributions from Kelly Oliver, Feder and Zakin, Rawlinson, Tina Chanter, Eva Plonowska Ziarek, Drucilla Cornell, and John Caputo. These collections, representing a complex diversity of feminist approaches and issues, are by no means uncritical of Derrida's work, in some cases attributing essentializing, dualist, and re-naturalizing tendencies to it, while in other cases finding its difference full of ethical promise.

The scholarship of Drucilla Cornell has contributed importantly to the ongoing assessment of deconstruction's significance for feminist, ethical, and legal studies. Cornell was one of the organizers of the *Deconstruction and the Possibility of Justice* conference held in October 1989 at the Benjamin N. Cardozo School of Law. A collection published in 1992 under the conference title includes Derrida's presentation, ("Force of Law: The 'Mystical Foundation of Authority'") along with thirteen other papers that examine deconstruction in relation to justice, law, and politics (Cornell, Rosenfeld, and Gray Carlson 1992). Building on the paper she presented at the Cardozo conference, Cornell went on to publish a book-length study, *The Philosophy of the Limit* (1992), which engages the work of both Derrida and Levinas (alongside that of Jacques Lacan); contends with the "postmodern" label; foregrounds the importance of questions of sexual difference to problems of justice and legal interpretation; and reads the potential of Derrida's work for transforming legal and ethical norms. Two other of her book publications, both drawing on Derrida, are also essential to feminist and legal studies: *Transformations: Recollective Imagination and Sexual Difference* (1993) and *Beyond Accommodation: Ethical Feminism, Deconstruction, and the Law* (1999).

David Carroll suggests in "'Remains' of Algeria: Justice, Hospitality, Politics" (2006) that traces (remains) of Derrida's Algerian past can be found in his works where questions of justice are at issue, where discussion turns to immigration, refugees, political exiles, all those who are foreigners in a foreign land. For Carroll, Derrida's ethics of unconditional hospitality to the other—the inferior, alien, threatening, unnamed, non-people, people with limited rights—constitutes a disturbance to all oppositional hierarchies and to any ethics or politics that is grounded in them. Derrida's "figural" relation to Judaism is at stake here, for as Mark Dooley and Liam Kavanagh note in a recent study, the figure of the Jew in Derrida's work, *contra* Hegel, "represents all those who are exiled and do not belong" (Dooley and Kavanagh 2007, 13). Hospitality and exile are thus examined together in studies of national, racial, and sexual difference that work from the *Geschlecht* papers, *Glas*, "Racism's Last Word," and other of Derrida's texts. Geoffrey Galt Harpham in *Shadows of Ethics* (1999) suggests something of the disturbance such work involves, which, in every case, requires a rethinking of *responsibility* (see Keenan 1997; and on the relation between hospitality, responsibility and religion in Derrida's work, see the 2002 study by Hent de Vries, *Religion and Violence*).

Nowhere is responsibility more at issue than in Derrida's writing on the animal question. His groundbreaking work here was very much in process and cut short by his death. Many studies have resulted from this work (see for example, Baker 2003; Calarco 2002, 2005; Lawlor 2007; Lippit 1998; Wood 2004), one important recent volume being Leonard Lawlor's *This Is Not Sufficient* (2007), which is both an accomplished study of Derrida's writing on animality, and an indicator of how much remains to be done on this question.

Religion and philosophy

In some ways, it is arbitrary to separate out a section on religion and philosophy from the other areas listed above, all of which put religion in relation to philosophy. But we have not yet mentioned a sizeable literature that
has developed over the past twenty years in a field that broaches religio-
philosophical, or philosophico-religious, concerns arising from the study
of Derrida's work. Some of this literature takes up theological issues (e.g.
Hart 1990), and some of it, notwithstanding Derrida's disclaimers, delves
into the relation between deconstruction and negative theology (e.g. Coward and Foshay 1992). Much writing has been done on a religious- or
theology-phenomenology relationship in the texts of Derrida, for example
on the question whether Derrida's thinking of the Other "makes room for
God," as Rodolphe Gasché puts it in "God, for Example" (Gasché 1994,
161; on "the Other" in Derrida, see also Gasché's 1986 study, *The Tain of
the Mirror*). Although the point is contested, some of this literature argues
for a religious or theological "turn," not only in recent phenomenology (in
the work of Jean-Luc Marion, for example), but in Derrida's "late" writing
as well. Bruce Ellis Benson makes this case in *Graven Ideologies* (2002),
suggesting that, "already deeply influenced by Levinas in the 1960s," Derrida became increasingly concerned during the last two decades of the
twentieth century with "transcendence as worked out in ethics and religion, no doubt in part due to the influence of his former student Marion"
(Benson 2002, 10). Earlier than Benson, Hent de Vries in *Philosophy and
the Turn to Religion* (1999), working with Derrida's "later" writings, posits a
"turn" to religion in modern philosophy, particularly in phenomenology.

In quite a different vein, philosophical work on the "turn" to religion
in Derrida's texts might suggest that religion is far from over, that the
"deconstruction of Christianity" in which he engaged remains a task for
much future research. This deconstruction is larger than any other to which
Derrida's work opens, Leonard Lawlor suggests in *The Implications of
Immanence: Toward a New Concept of Life* (2006), and it necessarily
involves a movement back from Christianity to Judaism and Islam, traditions that would otherwise be ignored as important components of the
West (Lawlor 2006, 158 n. 12; see also 31). In this case, to engage Derrida
on the "turn" to religion is to take up the notion of the Abrahamic, which is of
Islamic origin, Gil Anidjar notes in his Introduction to *Acts of Religion*, and
which deconstructs or "dissociates" the "dividing movement around which
'Europe' —and religion—constitutes itself" (Anidjar 2002, 7).

Return-to-religion discussions marginalize Islam, Derrida points out in
"Faith and Knowledge," the paper he presented in 1994 on the Isle of

Capri. We have noted that the Capri seminar included neither women nor representation from Islam. At the opening of the volume that came out of the 2002 conference in Toronto on "Derrida and Religion: Other Testaments," Yvonne Sherwood and Kevin Hart point out that the membership at the Toronto conference was "only slightly broader than the colloquium on Capri," for although the event included women, it was otherwise confined to Christians and Jews, without representation from Islam, or from Hinduism, Buddhism, or any other religious groups (Sherwood and Hart, 2005, 15). If the 2002 Toronto event serves as an example, scholarly discussion of Derrida's work in relation to religion, or to its return, has yet to really open the field, even to what Anidjar calls the "Abrahamic." Anidjar's "Introduction" to *Acts of Religion* addresses this issue provocatively, and other "world religions" studies have now begun to emerge (see for example, Almond 2002; 2004).

As a final note, Derrida's work is contributing to the field of religion through a range of comparative research. For one example, Hent de Vries, in "Anti-Babel: The 'Mystical Postulate' in Benjamin, de Certeau, and Derrida" (1992), explores similarities and differences between Derrida and Walter Benjamin's views of language (by way of a detour through de Certeau), finding Derrida the less "metaphysical" and "eschatological" of the two thinkers. Dana Hollander's *Exemplarity and Chosenness* (2008) brings Derrida's work together with that of Franz Rosenzweig (1886–1929), examining the universal claims of philosophy in relation to claims of Jewish exemplarity. Leonard Lawlor's work on *Derrida and Husserl* (2002) adds to a growing deconstruction-and-phenomenology field. And as we have mentioned along the way, much comparative research relates Derrida's work to that of Levinas, Augustine, Plato, Heidegger, and other thinkers of the Western religio-philosophical, or philosophico-religious, tradition (for one example of a Derrida-Aquinas study, see Young 2007).

Chapter 7

Legacies

In the plural

The Oxford English Dictionary defines a "legacy" as a "gift," something left in a will, handed down by a predecessor. We opened this book by suggesting that this is not Derrida's understanding of inheritance. It is never a given, he said, but always a task. The task is incalculable. And in this sense, a legacy is not a gift that can be submitted to an economy of return. It is open, and will always remain so, which means that we will never be finished reading, receiving and responding to, tradition. Nor we will ever finish reading Derrida. Here is one of his great legacies to us. From Derrida, as Eduardo Cadava says, we have inherited "the obligation to think about the nature of inheritance" (Cadava 2005, 472).

In his remarks on inheritance that we recall at the opening of this book, Derrida reminds us that, above all, tradition cannot be gathered. Inheritance is about legacies in the plural. We cannot conclude, then, with a summary condensation of Derrida's legacy. There are too many legacies to consider, more than one writer or one discipline can "rein in." Here is another of Derrida's legacies to us: sovereignty is a phantasm. No academic discipline can survive as a bounded entity. Hospitality to the other is the requirement of responsible reading and writing. It is the requirement of your research as a student of religion. Derrida's legacies exceed the grasp of any particular discipline, and as we have noted in this book,

---

The chapter at a glance:

Legacies: All of Derrida's work seeks to understand what the legacies of tradition might be. This chapter asks what we might inherit from Derrida.

---

his work calls for ongoing questioning of such categories as "genre" and "discipline." Derrida's texts engage the legacies of the theological and religious traditions of the West, but never by circumscribing religion as a field unto itself.

Over the course of his career, countless conferences and proceedings publications were given to Derrida's work, some of which we mention in this book. Since his death, many more events, conference proceedings publications, and special issues of journals, have attempted to address the question of his legacies. Here, we outline only some of these "legacies" initiatives, offerings toward "legacies in the plural." These works of impossible mourning provide a glimpse into Derrida's inheritance as "yet-to-come." Once asked whether what we have inherited from Plato and Hegel is still provocative, Derrida replied: "Oh yes, I always have the feeling that, despite centuries of reading, these texts remain untouched, withdrawn into a reserve, still to come" (PT 82). Readers of Derrida can, and will continue to say, the same of his texts. ~~but not same~~

With the news of his death on October 8, 2004, scholars and students around the world began asking what it means "to follow" Derrida. Books and numerous individual papers were published. But rather than single these out, we might note some of the collaborative publications that came out of conferences and journal special issues. For example, in March 2005, *PMLA* issued a "Forum: The Legacy of Jacques Derrida," to which nineteen academics contributed texts on Derrida's legacies. A special issue of the journal *Epoché*, edited by Pleshette De Armitt and Kas Saghafi, appeared in the Spring of 2006, *An Entrusted Responsibility: Reading and Remembering Jacques Derrida*, which includes twelve essays, in addition to a Letter from the Editors, a brief contribution, "Consolation, Desolation," from Jean-Luc Nancy, and a text by Derrida himself, "A Europe of Hope." The journal *Research In Phenomenology* published a special 2006 issue, *Memorials For Jacques Derrida*, edited by John Sallis and James Risser, and including fifteen papers. In October 2006, to commemorate the second anniversary of his death, *Mosaic: a journal for the interdisciplinary study of literature* hosted an international and interdisciplinary conference, involving close to two hundred participants, "Following Derrida: Legacies." The conference saw the launch of *After Derrida*, a special issue of *Mosaic* edited by Dawne McCance and including fourteen essays on Derrida's legacies. As well, McCance edited a special conference proceedings issue of *Mosaic* in June 2007, *Following Derrida: Legacies,* which includes twenty essays, contributions from across the disciplines, on Derrida's legacies. Ian Balfour edited a special issue of *The South Atlantic Quarterly* in the Spring of 2007, *Late Derrida*, a collection of eight essays in addition to Balfour's introduction. Also in 2007, *Critical Inquiry* published a special issue, *The Late Derrida*, edited by W.J.T. Mitchell and Arnold I. Davidson and including eleven contributions in addition to an interview with Derrida, his text "A Certain Impossible Possibility of Saying the Event," and the "Final Words" that were written by him and spoken by his son at his graveside.

These collections would be good places to begin to glimpse what it means to inherit Derrida as a key thinker of religion, whose legacies for this field of study move across the disciplines. Among the many topics taken up in the collections (including autoimmunity, memory, forgiveness, spectrality, chance, philosophy, temporality, speech act theory, Europe, mourning, the future, drawing, art, the gift, translation, religion, suffering, friendship, animality, sovereignty, presence, the university, faith, law), none remains unmarked by what Derrida called "undecidability," or *khôra*, which is but another name for this, one of his many "figures" of the "undecidable." We have suggested in this book that "undecidability" may be the key of Derrida's key contributions to the study of religion, akin to his thinking of an originary faith that cannot be named or contained by a university discipline, or by any discourse or institution. "There are no clean margins around the world for Derrida, no well demarcated beginning or end, no absolute *arche*, no tidy *telos*," John Caputo suggests in *After Derrida*. "For Derrida, what exists—the distinct and particular things that make up our world, the narratives that constitute our histories—is inscribed in a medium or milieu or desert place that is older than the world or life, older than nature or history, that is older than time and eternity, older than Europe or philosophy or science, or Judaism and Christianity. That is what he is calling *khôra*" (Caputo 2006, 97).

Glossary

Animality: Much of Derrida's work analyses and questions Western discourses of *animality* (from the Latin *animalis*, having the breath of life), that is, discourses that define and defend a limit "between the living being called 'human' and the one called 'animal'" (R 151).

Autoimmunity: Derrida refers to this as the "strange behavior" by which a living system (self, entity, institution, community, nation-state), "in quasi-*suicidal* fashion, 'itself' works to destroy its own protection, to immunize itself *against* its 'own' immunity" (PTT 94). One example of this would be a religion's (e.g., Roman Catholicism's) attempts to immunize itself against the telecommunications, technoscience, and technical reason that, while perceived as threats, already work from within religion, and, in today's world, are necessary to its survival.

Deconstruction: "To get ready for this coming of the other is what can be called deconstruction" (PSY 39).

Differance: A sort of inscription prior to writing, a never-present "place" or "space" of inscription like *khôra*, differance would be "the movement of play" that "produces" and differs, differences. "This does not mean that the differance which produces differences is before them in a simple and in itself unmodified and indifferent present. Differance is the nonfull, nonsimple 'origin'; it is the structured and differing origin of differences" (SP 141).

Eschatology: From Greek words meaning "last" and "discourse," eschatology concerns last things, the final destiny of an individual, community, or history. It is tied closely to *messianism*, also to *teleology*, teaching or writing on final causes.

Geschlecht: A title word in three published (and one unpublished) papers examining "the animal" question in Heidegger (and questions of difference in general), *Geschlecht* is a "practically untranslatable" term that can mean generation, genus, gender, sex, race, family, stock, species, or tongue.

Khôra: As Derrida reads it from Plato's *Timaeus*, *khôra* "is" a "place of inscription" that exceeds discursive capture, precedes metaphysics, and belongs to no paradigm. This is one of Derrida's "undecidables."

The messianic: "This would be the opening to the future or to the coming of the other as the advent of justice, but without horizon of expectation and without prophetic prefiguration" (FK 56). The messianic is distinct from messianism of any type.

Metaphysics: In her "Translator's Preface" to *Of Grammatology*, Gayatri Chakravorty Spivak suggests that "Derrida uses the word 'metaphysics' very simply as shorthand for any science of presence" (OG xxi). As this definition rightly suggests, metaphysics is not limited to philosophy, but discursive practice within the Western tradition for which essential being is determined as *presence*. Another shorthand used for this term is "metaphysics of presence." The epoch or tradition of Western metaphysics can be said to begin with Plato's positing of a fundamental distinction between the intelligible and sensible realms.

Pharmakon: a term that Derrida finds in Plato's *Phaedrus* and reads (against Plato's attempts to confine it within an oppositional either/or) as resistant to any philosopheme, and, far from being governed by binary oppositions, as what "opens up their very possibility without letting itself be comprehended by them" (D 103).

Phonocentrism: In his readings of Husserl and of the tradition of metaphysics overall, Derrida refers to phonocentrism as the effacement of the signifier in a transcendental unity of voice and idea. Phonocentrism is a *logocentrism* that posits a relationship of essential and immediate proximity between *logos* (mind) and *phonè* (OG 11). It makes phonetic speech/ writing the medium of the "metaphysical, scientific, technical, and economic adventure of the West" (OG 10).

Sign: As defined by Ferdinand de Saussure and as analysed by Derrida in *Of Grammatology*, the sign implies a distinction between the signifier (the material element, the sensible, written, medium) and the signified (idea, concept). In traditional theory of the sign, the written part, the signifier, is always taken to be technical and representative. Derrida says that the sign belongs broadly to the epoch of metaphysics, more narrowly to the epoch of Christian creationism (OG 13).

Sovereignty: As in la Fontaine's fable of "The Wolf and the Lamb," sovereignty is based on the claim that "might is right." It represents the "phantasm" that the sovereign entity (self or nation-state) is the locus of undivided power, authorized by itself to make its own law and to use force in its own self-interest. Derrida says that sovereignty is a form of secularized theology.

Specter: A name for the "trace" that haunts "truth," for what "disjoins" claims to presence, for what, in its movement of coming-and-going, introduces an asymmetry into every discourse of the same, the specter (revenant) is a "figure" of the other.

Trace: Not a sign and not a presence, the trace "dislocates, displaces, and refers beyond itself." Effacement constitutes it, "establishes the trace in a change of place and makes it disappear in its appearing" (SP 156).

Undecidability: The other to which Derrida's work opens and responds is incalculable, escapes all nomination and programming, is not determinable as either this or that, or as both this and that. This undecidable other, which goes by many "names," allows "the adventure or the event of the entirely other to come. Of an entirely other that can no longer be confused with the God or the Man of ontotheology or with any of the figures of this configuration (the subject, consciousness, the unconscious, the self, man or woman, and so on)" (PSY 46).

References

Almond, Ian. 2002. The honesty of the perplexed: Derrida and Ibn 'Arabi on "bewilderment." *Journal of the American Academy of Religion* 70(3): 515–537.

Anidjar, Gil. 2002. Introduction: "Once More, Once More": Derrida, the Arab, the Jew. In Jacques Derrida, *Acts of Religion.* Ed. Gil Anidjar, 1–39. London: Routledge.

Baker, Steve. 2003. Philosophy in the Wild? Kac and Derrida on Animals and Responsibility. *New Formations* 49: 91–98.

Balfour, Ian, ed. 2007. *Late Derrida. The South Atlantic Quarterly* 106(2).

Bennington, Geoffrey. 1993. Derridabase. In *Jacques Derrida,* ed. Geoffrey Bennington and Jacques Derrida. Trans. Geoffrey Bennington. Chicago, IL: University of Chicago Press.

Benson, Bruce Ellis. 2002. *Graven ideologies: Nietzsche, Derrida and Marion on modern idolatry.* Downers Grove, IL: InterVarsity Press.

Bernasconi, Robert and Simon Critchley, eds. 1991. *Re-Reading Levinas.* Bloomington: Indiana University Press.

Cadava, Eduardo. 2005. "I would like to begin by remembering." In Forum: The Legacy of Jacques Derrida. *PMLA* 120(2): 471–472.

Calarco, Matthew. 2002. On the borders of Language and Death: Derrida and the Question of the Animal. *Angelaki* 7(2): 7–25.

———. 2005. "Another Insistence of Man": Prolegomena to the Question of the Animal in Derrida's Reading of Heidegger. *Human Studies* 28(3): 317–334.

Caputo, John D. 1987. *Radical Hermeneutics: Repetition, Deconstruction, and the Hermeneutic Project.* Bloomington: Indiana University Press.

———. 1997. *The Prayers and Tears of Jacques Derrida: Religion without Religion.* Bloomington: Indiana University Press.

2006   Before Creation: Derrida's Memory of God. *Mosaic* 39(3): 91–102.

Caputo, John D., Mark Dooley, and Michael J. Scanlon, eds. 2001. *Questioning God*. Bloomington: Indiana University Press.

Caputo, John D. and Michael J. Scanlon. 1999. *God, the Gift, and Postmodernism*. Bloomington: Indiana University Press.

———. 2005. *Augustine and Postmodernism: Confessions and Circumfession*. Bloomington: Indiana University Press.

Carroll, David. 2006. "Remains" of Algeria: Justice, Hospitality, Politics. *MLN* 121: 808–827.

Cixous, Hélène. 2004. *Portrait of Jacques Derrida as a Young Jewish Saint*. Trans. Beverley Bie Brahic. New York: Columbia University Press.

Cornell, Drucilla. 1992. *The Philosophy of the Limit*. London: Routledge.

———. 1993. *Transformations: Recollective Imagination and Sexual Difference*. London: Routledge.

———. 1999. *Beyond Accommodation: Ethical Feminism, Deconstruction, and the Law*. Lanham, MD: Rowman and Littlefield.

Cornell, Drucilla, Michel Rosenfeld, and David Gray Carlson, eds. 1992. *Deconstruction and the Possibility of Justice*. London: Routledge.

Coward, Harold G. 1990. *Derrida and Indian Philosophy*. Albany: State University of New York Press.

———. 1991. Speech versus Writing in Derrida and Bhartrhari. *Philosophy East and West* 41(2): 141–162.

Coward, Harold G. and Toby Foshay. 1992. *Derrida and Negative Theology*. Albany: State University of New York Press.

Critchley, Simon. 1992. *The Ethics of Deconstruction: Derrida and Levinas*. Oxford: Blackwell.

———. 1998. A Comment Upon Derrida's Reading of Hegel in *Glas*. In *Hegel After Derrida*, ed. Stuart Barnett, 197–226. London: Routledge.

Dallery, Arleen and Charles E. Scott. 1989. *The Question of the Other: Essays in Contemporary Continental Philosophy*. Albany: State University of New York Press.

De Armitt, Pleshette and Kas Saghafi, eds. 2006. An Entrusted Responsibility: Reading and Remembering Jacques Derrida. *Epoché: a journal for the history of philosophy* 10(2).

De Vries, Hent. 1992. Anti-Babel: The "Mystical Postulate" in Benjamin, de Certeau and Derrida. *MLN* 107(3): 441–477.

———. 1999. *Philosophy and the Turn to Religion*. Baltimore: The Johns Hopkins University Press.

————. 2002. *Religion and violence: philosophical perspectives from Kant to Derrida.* Baltimore: The Johns Hopkins University Press.

Dooley, Mark and Liam Kavanagh. 2007. *The Philosophy of Derrida.* Montréal: McGill-Queens University Press.

Feder, Ellen K., Mary C. Rawlinson and Emily Zakin, eds. 1997. *Derrida and Feminism. Reading the Question of Woman.* London: Routledge.

Fenves, Peter, ed. 1993. *Raising the Tone of Philosophy: Late Essays by Immanuel Kant, Transformative Critique by Jacques Derrida.* Baltimore: Johns Hopkins University Press.

Gadamer, Hans-Georg. 2004. *Truth and Method.* Trans. Joel Weinsheimer and Donald G. Marhsall. London: Continuum.

————. 1996. "Dialogues in Capri." Trans. Jason Gaiger. *Religion,* eds. Jacques Derridea and Gianni Vattimo. Stanford, CA: Stanford University Press.

Gasché, Rodolphe. 1986. *The Tain of the Mirror: Derrida and the Philosophy of Reflection.* Cambridge, MA: Harvard University Press.

————. 1994. *Inventions of Difference: On Jacques Derrida.* Cambridge, MA: Harvard University Press.

————. 2007. *Views and Interviews.* Aurora, CO: The Davies Group Publishers.

Grosz, Elizabeth. 1995. Ontology and Equivocation: Derrida's Politics of Sexual Difference. *Diacritics* 25(2): 114–124.

Habermas, Jürgen. 1990. *The Philosophical Discourse of Modernity.* Trans. Frederick G. Lawrence. Cambridge, MA: MIT Press.

Hart, Kevin. 1990. *The Trespass of the Sign: Deconstruction, Theology, and Philosophy.* New York: Cambridge University Press.

Handelman, Susan. 1982. *The Slayers of Moses: The Emergence of Rabbinic Interpretation in Modern Literary Theory.* Albany: State University of New York Press.

————. 1983. Jacques Derrida and the Heretic Hermeneutic. In *Displacement: Derrida and After,* ed. Mark Krupnick, 98–129. Bloomington: Indiana University Press.

Harpham, Geoffrey Galt. 1999. *Shadows of Ethics: Criticism and the Just Society.* Durham, NC: Duke University Press.

Heidegger, Martin. 1962. *Being and Time.* Trans. John Macquarrie and Edward Robinson. New York: Harper and Row.

Holland, Nancy J., ed. 1997. *Feminist Interpretations of Jacques Derrida.* University Park: Pennsylvania State University Press.

Hollander, Dana. 2008. *Exemplarity and Chosenness: Rosenzweig and Derrida on the Nation of Philosophy*. Stanford, CA: Stanford University Press.

Jameson, Fredric. 1984. Postmodernism, or the Cultural Logic of Late Capitalism. *New Left Review* 146: 53–92.

Joy, Morny. 1988. Derrida and Ricoeur: A Case of Mistaken Identity (And Difference). *The Journal of Religion* 68(4): 508–526.

Kamuf, Peggy. 2006. Composition Displacement. *MLN* 121: 872–892.

Keenan, Thomas. 1997. *Fables of Responsibility: Aberrations and Predicaments in Ethics and Politics*. Stanford, CA: Stanford University Press.

Krell, David Farrell. 2000. *The Purest of Bastards: Works of Mourning, Art, and Affirmation in the Thought of Jacques Derrida*. University Park: Pennsylvania University Press.

———. 2006. One, Two, Four—Yet Where Is the Third? A Note on Derrida's *Geschlecht* Series. In An Entrusted Responsibility: Reading and Remembering Jacques Derrida. *Epoché: a journal for the history of philosophy* 10(2): 341–357.

Lawlor, Leonard. 2002. *Derrida and Husserl: The Basic Problems of Phenomenology*. Bloomington: Indiana University Press.

———. 2006. *The Implications of Immanence: Toward a New Concept of Life*. New York: Fordham University Press.

———. 2007. *This Is Not Sufficient: An Essay on Animality and Human Nature in Derrida*. New York: Columbia University Press.

Leavey, John P., Jr. 1986. *Glassary*. Lincoln and London: University of Nebraska Press.

Lippit, Akira Mizuta. 1998. Magnetic Animal: Derrida, Wildlife, *Animetaphor*. *MLN* 113(5): 1111–1125.

Llewelyn, John. 2002. *Appositions of Jacques Derrida and Emmanuel Levinas*. Bloomington: Indiana University Press.

MacIntyre, Alasdair. 1981. *After Virtue: A Study in Moral Theory*. Notre Dame, IN: University of Notre Dame Press.

Marrati, Paola. 2005. *Genesis and Trace: Derrida Reading Husserl and Heidegger*. Stanford, CA: Stanford University Press.

McCance, Dawne. 1996. *Posts: Re Addressing the Ethical*. New York: State University of New York Press.

———, ed. 2006. *After Derrida*. A special issue of *Mosaic* 39(3).

———, ed. 2007. *Following Derrida: Legacies*. A special issue of *Mosaic* 40(2).

Michelfelder, Diane P. and Richard E. Palmer. 1989. *Dialogue and Deconstruction: The Gadamer-Derrida Encounter*. Albany: State University of New York Press.

Mitchell, W. J. T. and Arnold I. Davidson, eds. 2007. *The Late Derrida*: a special issue of *Critical Inquiry*. Chicago: University of Chicago Press.

Nass, Michael. 2003. *Taking on the Tradition: Jacques Derrida and the Legacies of Deconstruction*. Stanford, CA: Stanford University Press.

———. 2006. "One Nation… Indivisible": Jacques Derrida on the Autoimmunity of Democracy and the Sovereignty of God. *Research in Phenomenology* 36: 15–44.

PMLA. 2005. "Forum: The Legacy of Jacques Derrida." 120(2): 464–494.

Ricoeur, Paul. 1976. *Interpretation Theory*. Fort Worth: Texas Christian University Press.

———. 1977. *The Rule of Metaphor*. Trans. Robert Czerny, with Kathleen McLaughlin and John Costello, S.J. Toronto: University of Toronto Press.

———. 1981. *Hermeneutics and the Human Sciences: Essays on language, action and interpretation*. Trans. and ed. John B. Thompson. Cambridge: Cambridge University Press.

Robbins, Jill. 1995. Circumcising Confession: Derrida, Autobiography, Judaism. *Diacritics* 25(4): 20–38.

Royle, Nicholas. 2003. *Jacques Derrida*. London: Routledge.

Sallis, John. 2008. *The Verge of Philosophy*. Chicago: University of Chicago Press.

Sallis, John, and James Risser. 2006. Memorials for Jacques Derrida: A tribute to Jacques Derrida. *Research in Phenomenology* 36(1). Leiden: Brill Academic Publishers.

Sherwood, Yvonne and Kevin Hart, eds. 2005. *Derrida and Religion: Other Testaments*. New York: Routledge.

Silverman, Hugh J. and Don Ihde, eds. 1985. *Hermeneutics and Deconstruction*. Albany: State University of New York Press.

Silverman, Hugh J. 1994. *Textualities: Between Hermeneutics and Deconstruction*. London: Routledge.

Spivak, Gayatri. 1995. Ghostwriting. *Diacritics* 25(2): 65–84.

Sprinker, Michael, ed. 1999. *Ghostly Demarcations: A Symposium on Jacques Derrida's Specters of Marx*. London: Verso.

Taylor, Mark C. 1984. *Erring: A Postmodern A/Theology*. Chicago, IL:

University of Chicago Press.

————. 1987. *Altarity*. Chicago, IL: University of Chicago Press.

————. 1993. *Nots.* Chicago, IL: University of Chicago Press.

Thomassen, Lasse, ed. 2006. *The Derrida-Habermas Reader.* Chicago, IL: University of Chicago Press.

Winquist, Charles E. and John D. Caputo. 1990. Derrida and the Study of Religion. *Religious Studies Review* 16(1): 19–25.

Wise, Christopher. 2001. Deconstruction and Zionism: Jacques Derrida's *Specters of Marx. Diacritics* 31(1): 56–72.

Wood, David. 2004. Thinking With Cats. In *Animal Philosophy: Ethics and Identity,* eds. Peter Atterton and Matthew Calarco, 129–144. London: Continuum.

Wyschogrod, Edith. 1990. *Saints and Postmodernism.* Chicago, IL: University of Chicago Press.

Young, William W. 2007. *The politics of praise: naming God and friendship in Aquinas and Derrida.* Burlington, VT : Ashgate.

Index

A

Adami, Valerio 3
Almond, Ian 103
Althusser, Louis 12
Anidjar, Gil 4, 92, 102, 103
animality 54, 61–64, 68, 95, 101, 107, 109
aporia 19, 76, 86
Aristotle 3, 44, 78
Armour, Ellen 100
Artaud, Antonin 17, 41
Aucouturier, Marguerite 8, 12
Augustine of Hippo 3, 71, 82, 83, 95, 103
autobiography 3, 72, 81–82, 98
autoimmunity 39–40, 73–74, 77–79, 107, 109
à-venir 35, 38, *see also* "to come"

B

Baker, Steve 101
Balfour, Ian 106
Bass, Alan 17
Bataille, Georges 17
Baudelaire, Charles 69
Benjamin, Walter 3, 17, 33, 86, 103
Bennington, Geoffrey 9–10, 11, 14, 88, 89, 91, 95
Benson, Bruce Ellis 102
Benveniste, Émile 69
Bernasconi, Robert 100
Birmingham, Peg 100
Birnbaum, Jean vii
Borradori, Giovanna 97
Brault, Pascale-Anne 71

C

Cadava, Eduardo 105
Calarco, Matthew 101

Capelle, Philippe 95
Caputo, John 4, 24, 55, 81, 83, 89, 90, 92, 93, 94, 95, 97, 98, 99, 100, 107
carno-phallogocentrism 26, 52
Carroll, David 101
Celan, Paul 3
Chanter, Tina 100
Christianity 1, 62, 66, 69, 74, 107
circumcision 9, 87–89
Cixous, Hélène 1, 43
Cohen, Hermann 86
Cornell, Drucilla 100–01
Coward, Harold G. 93, 102
Critchley, Simon 52, 99–100

D

Dallery, Arleen 100
David, Catherine 20
Davidson, Arnold 107
deconstruction 1–2, 10–11, 15, 17, 19–24, 28, 34–35, 36, 38, 41, 44, 52–53, 55, 56, 58, 77–78, 90, 97–99, 100–01, 102–03, 109
De Armitt, Pleshette 106
Deleuze, Gilles 1
de Man, Paul 35–36
democracy 34, 40, 75, 77–79, 85, 95
de Montaigne, Michel 34
Derrida, Aimé 7–8
de Saussure, Ferdinand 3, 17, 25, 110
Descartes, René 3, 17, 41, 44, 59
de Tocqueville, Alexis 79
de Vries, Hent 84, 95, 101, 102, 103
différance 4, 24, 26–30, 109
Dionysius 3, 30
Dooley, Mark 92, 93, 94, 101
Dufourmantelle, Anne 36

Lightning Source UK Ltd.
Milton Keynes UK
02 June 2010

155017UK00001B/35/P